12 DISCIPLES

12 DISCIPLES

YOUNG PEOPLE'S STORIES OF CRISIS AND FAITH

ANDY FLANNAGAN + ANNE CALVER

Halesowen, UK

MONARCH
BOOKS

Oxford, UK & Grand Rapids, Michigan, USA

First published in the UK in 2007 by Monarch Books
(a publishing imprint of Lion Hudson plc),
Mayfield House, 256 Banbury Road, Oxford OX2 7DH
Tel: +44 (0) 1865 302750   Fax: +44 (0) 1865 302757
Email: monarch@lionhudson.com
www.lionhudson.com

Distributed by:
UK: Marston Book Services Ltd, PO Box 269, Abingdon, Oxon OX14 4YN.
USA: Kregel Publications, PO Box 2607, Grand Rapids, Michigan 49501.

ISBN: 978-1-85424-801-5 (UK)
ISBN: 978-0-8254-6171-2 (USA)

Unless otherwise stated, Scripture quotations are taken from the
Holy Bible, New International Version, © 1973, 1978, 1984
by the International Bible Society. Used by permission of
Hodder and Stoughton Ltd. All rights reserved.

The text paper used in this book has been made from wood
independently certified as having come from sustainable forests.

British Library Cataloguing Data
A catalogue record for this book is available from the British Library.

Printed in Malta by Gutenberg Press.

Contents

Foreword

There are those who say that this generation of teenagers has no interest in spiritual realities and are turned off to God. Nothing could be further from the truth! Teenagers have deep spiritual longings and are hungry to hear from those who know how to make God real to them. There is a restlessness among them that emerges from an unarticulated craving for that which can give them a sense of affirmation that they have infinite worth. They are looking for that which can give meaning and significance to their lives. In short, any social psychologist will readily acknowledge that there is a prevalent hunger for God and meaning that permeates the youth culture.

Unfortunately the church has great difficulty satisfying the hungers and meeting the needs that young people have for being connected with those spiritual realities which are beyond themselves. We in the church usually do not speak their language nor understand how they view the world, but it's not our fault! We are who we are! We live in a different world than most contemporary young people. We are like aliens to them, and they to us. Their music; their dress; their vocabulary; their value systems – are all strange to us. The church is the church and the youth culture is the youth culture, and it might be said that seldom do the twain meet.

All is not lost, however. There are those youth workers who recognise this disconnect and sense a call to be "in the gap", so to speak.

These are "bridge" people who, on the one hand, love and understand the subculture of the church and, on the other hand, love and understand those teenagers who make up the somewhat countercultural group that we older folks find beyond our understanding. One such array of Christians who form a bridge between the church and teenage world are those who serve with Youth For Christ – a parachurch movement composed of young missionaries who are especially adept at bringing the message of the church to a new generation of young people who are more than ready to listen to the gospel story, if only it would be presented in ways that they can grasp. That is what Youth For Christ does. Its leaders and workers are deeply committed to expressing the eternal truth that was revealed in Jesus Christ. They do it in ways that are functionally fit for the emerging culture in which most teenagers today are living their lives. This book is about those teenagers, and vividly defines the cravings of their souls for spiritual realities.

You will find the pages that follow a compilation of stories of young people who find religion strange and distant but who are, nevertheless, desirous of the essence of the biblical message of Christ and his salvation story. They are stories of how many of them have stumbled towards the answers to the riddles of their lives and how they are sometimes met by persons, such as those who are in the ministries of Youth For Christ, who can help them along their way.

It is not that these YFC youth workers have some special handle on the truth, or offer us some new revelation from God. Instead, it is simply that they are able to contextualise the eternal truths of God in the culture in which most modern (or should I say post-modern) young people live. These special missionaries make it a primary principle not just to preach at young people but also to affirm their worth as persons created in the image of God. They work hard to convince teenagers that the one who created them has purposes especially designed for each of their lives. Those who work in the Youth For Christ ministries model for young people lifestyles that do not negate the true identities of young people but, instead, demonstrate how each and every teenager can actualise the ultimate yearnings of their hearts in ways that glorify God.

What you will find described in the stories that follow is that such movements and organisations present some of the best agencies to bridge the gap between an alienated youth and a church that too often has lost touch with those who live in this teenage subculture. Youth For Christ is a brilliant instrument whereby young people can be brought into the church. What is more, it is well aware that if it doesn't deliver young converts into the church then all the good that might have been achieved through its efforts will soon fade away.

I hope that what follows will give evidence of some ways in which young people have become sensitised to God through Youth For Christ. The techniques and methodologies YFC uses for connecting with the hearts and souls of young people are as old as the Bible and yet are still relevant to the modern "rock and rap" culture of contemporary teenagers. So reach out and get a taste of where young people are coming from, and where – by the grace of God – they can go with the right kind of guidance.

Tony Campolo, Ph.D.
Eastern University, St. Davids, PA. USA

3-story

In 1 Corinthians 15, Paul says he was the least of the Apostles. It would be true to say that sometimes, if not all the time, I feel just like that. Not that I would claim to be an apostle, but I certainly feel the least. Paul actually felt he had been nabbed, or even accosted, by God, and that Jesus messed up a very ordinary life in an extraordinary way, transforming it into a dynamic journey with the living God.

The day was ordinary in the sense of any day – and took place in the suburbs of London in a place called Borehamwood. My family had moved there from Hackney, my dad being a Fleet Street printer, my mum being a tailor, who produced amazing clothes. My brother and I attended different schools. On this particular day in question when I rode my bike to school, it was the same as any other day – maybe this day would change every other day? Maybe there is a God in heaven who directs our paths more than we might think, even when we are totally unaware of his leading or direction.

The lesson was French, Miss Hagins was trying to teach us the phrase 'the cat was on the mat' – which to me seemed totally irrelevant, because it had nothing to do with my world, or life for that matter – and, who cares if the cat was on the mat? I had been moved to sit next to Dave, and my focus had shifted to him. I was pretty interested in getting his story as he was the only one in school who went to church. The church was not an impressive building, no stained glass windows, no steeple – just a hall actually, but he went to a youth group in this hall and seemed to have fun. He was really keen for me to go and to feel a part of the group. I never normally went to church, none of my family did, although my dad had been in the choir as a lad because he was paid a bit for weddings, funerals and some special Sundays. Dave was different to me – a bit of a geek or a nerd really, not my type of person.

But Dave talked about a relationship with God – that he had asked Jesus into his heart, and it had not only changed him, but through him his brother and his mum had changed (although his dad had not changed). Therefore, I was all ears to get the story. I got a little nervous when he asked about my life, but I was more intrigued to hear how God had changed his life. I was fascinated and focused, but the next thing I knew was that the French teacher was standing right over me asking me to repeat a phrase. However I had already 'checked out' – I was in another world – no, the cat was not on the mat – and the teacher clearly knew it! Was God alive? Is Jesus real? Could he change lives today? This had no comparison with French. This was a far bigger subject, with some amazing consequences.

I did go to the youth club – there were further amazing stories – some interesting people, all of whom were claiming the same thing. I was cynical, I questioned, I was critical. These people were not perfect,

11

but they were convinced. There was a uniqueness about each story, but there was also a similarity. Their stories actually made it all real to me because their lives were part of something bigger – the story of God. Their stories seemed to have a divine connection. It seemed as if I was becoming a part of this because I was connected to Dave, resulting in my starting to connect to the God he knew. Mystical and strange, I know, but as a teenager these things seemed utterly real and amazing.

The question that now faced me was what I was now supposed to do? I definitely wasn't religious. I definitely didn't want that label, but our three stories (mine, Dave's and God's) seemed to be joining up. Would it be possible and credible that Jesus could change my life too? That's why, on a beach in Polseath, South Devon, with people of my own age with those same connections, I discovered that connection for myself.

What I have realised is that we all love a good story, but as that story becomes a part of life things change. The connection with the big story of God changed everything for me. It is an amazing way to live.

So, on an ordinary day and at an ordinary moment, things shifted to my taking part in an extraordinary, amazing, dynamic journey.

This book contains many more stories of young people on similar, but unique journeys. Whether you see yourself as the least or the greatest makes no difference. I am grateful for the work that Andy and Anne have done in telling these stories, and for Andy's commentaries on Peter and the work of YFC. Let these stories arrest you, challenge you and change you.

Roy Crowne
National Director, British Youth For Christ

Introduction

12 Disciples

You are about to meet 12 remarkable individuals. You've probably heard of one of them, but the others will be total strangers.

Their stories together form a journey of faith, with each individual representing a different stage of that journey. So we will be privileged to glimpse moments of first contact, first challenge, first doubts, calling, first use of gifting, first disappointment etc. It is a record of post-modern pilgrims' progress. Their roller coaster stories are aligned with the roller coaster story of Simon Peter, highlighting the similarities of some of the highs and lows of following this man called Jesus.

Our hope is that you will take the time to not only read their stories, but also journey with them, gleaning wisdom and encouragement from their lives. That way you may see the points at which your story and theirs fit together in the context of 'the big story' of God.

For various reasons, including safeguarding privacy and family wishes, names, locations and sometimes other specifics of stories have been changed. Those involved have however approved the finished copy and have agreed that the changes in no way dilute the integrity of what happened in each of the stories.

We have avoided the temptation to tell the whole story of each young person's life, but we instead focus in on their most significant moments, similar to the way that Matthew, Mark, Luke and John tell the story of Simon Peter. Each of these moments are merely a stage on the journey of faith, as they were for the man who would become the rock on which the church was built.

We want to express our heartfelt thanks to all the young people who agreed to be interviewed in the process of drawing these stories together. We gratefully appreciated your honesty and willingness to share your stories with the wider world. We don't take that vulnerability for granted. Thank you.

We also must thank the YFC Staff, youth leaders and other friends who pointed us in the direction of these remarkable young people. In many of these situations, your investment in these young people has been the difference between a happy and sad ending to these stories, so we hope that they will encourage you too.

There is much gritty reality here. There has been no editing of stories to remove unpleasant sections in an attempt to do a good PR job for Christianity. These authentically lived lives do that on their own, in an age where young people are looked down upon as a problem to be sorted out, rather than the potential engines of a hopeful future. They have reinforced my belief that there is "good news" to be told and as Youth For Christ, it is our privilege and duty to tell it.

Andy Flannagan

1 Pre-flight Checks

Gemma

'For what we are about to receive, may the Lord make us truly thankful. Amen.'

Gemma laughed at the thought of giving thanks for the hospital food that lay before her, but she couldn't look at a meal without hearing the echo of those words.

Her mind went tumbling backwards – she was reluctantly joining hands with her brothers and sisters around the family dinner table. It had always annoyed her when her Dad prayed. Having to wait while staring down at the crispy roast potatoes and smelling her Mum's thick red-wine-and-onion gravy was pure torture. What was the point in the praying bit anyway? It happened every mealtime without fail, and sometimes it went on for so long that she would deliberately open her eyes and smirk at her brothers and sisters, checking to see if anyone really bought this stuff.

God had always seemed like a distant relative to her – someone who kept being mentioned in family life but whom she had no real attachment to. When her parents spoke about God, Gemma chose not to engage in the discussion and did her best to shift the conversation elsewhere. She could cope with the word 'God', but hearing the name 'Jesus' made her feel distinctly uncomfortable. She found it a bit 'in-your-face', and wondered why they couldn't just stick to 'God'. It wasn't simply blissful ignorance. She had heard many stories about him and remembered the colourful paperbacks about people like Jonah and John the Baptist that she had pored over as a young child. She remembered singing about the foolish man who built a house on sand. Who in their right mind would lay foundations on a beach? How stupid he was, but how happy she used to be when the house fell flat and everyone was permitted, for a few moments, to make as much noise as they pleased.

A faint smile of memory appeared between the sheets of her straight brown hair, then disappeared quickly as she realized where she was. In this magnolia maternity ward, the pretty party girl was nowhere to be seen, and she was just another teenage pregnancy statistic. Struggling to deal with the reality of what lay before her, she hastily encouraged her mind to drift off again.

She thought back to the point when she had realized that other families were different. They didn't have to pray before dinner. Their conversations didn't embarrass them in front of their friends. She began to wonder why God was part of their family, and if he was really there at all.

Surely it was just a Father Christmas scenario – something that you grow out of when you realize that life is hard and truth is tough.

Something had shifted in Gemma the day before. Worries about the Caesarean section had dissipated when her best mate Mel had visited. Gemma bathed in the warm glow of happiness and excitement that her friend was exuding. 'Having this baby will be a turning-point for you,' Mel had said in a loaded fashion. Wasn't that stating the obvious? But her words had bounced around Gemma's head for the rest of the day.

Now, lying quietly on the bed, her mind drifted back to her family. In the last few months she had watched her siblings, one by one, decide to give this 'God thing' a go and had seen their lives change dramatically. It was crazy to think how swiftly John had quit heroin, married his pregnant girlfriend and begun a whole new life. What is more, he had emerged from rehab determined to rise to the challenges that he was going to have to face. Having ended an unhealthy relationship with her long-term boyfriend, Gemma's sister Rachel seemed to have a new-found sense of freedom and passion for life. Meanwhile, Gemma had watched from the sidelines, happy for *their* happiness but suspicious of change, and determined, in her words, to 'live life to the full'. Religion would not stop *her* doing whatever she wanted.

Three days later Gemma found herself at home with a baby boy. Sam's arrival had turned her life upside down. Looking after a newborn was exhausting enough without the added difficulty of recovering from major surgery. And the birth had unleashed an explosion of questions she couldn't shake off. 'How can two human beings create another human being? What triggers the current that starts a heartbeat that begins a new life? How could the egg that produced this baby have been stored in me before I was born?' It was overwhelming. 'This is all too beautiful and amazing,' she conceded as she picked up Sam. 'There *has* to be a God.'

This state of mind was short-lived, as she noticed the increasing numbness in the bottom of her spine. Fear crippled her meandering thoughts. Remembering the epidural and the doctor's words of warning, she was filled with dread. Without hesitating, she began to pray. She wasn't sure if God was listening or if he knew her or cared about her, but almost as soon as the words had left her mouth she felt peaceful. And when she reflected back on it a few months later, she observed how quickly her back had felt better.

But whilst Sam was an incredible gift, he also proved to be a real handful, and with Gemma and her boyfriend Jack also planning their wedding, all thoughts of God were pushed into the background. That is, until her next trip to the hospital.

Gemma's Gran was very ill. She hadn't been herself since her husband's death, but Gemma could never have imagined that the fall and subsequent infection would take her so close to the edge. Gran had been 'Gran' to hundreds of people, and although Gemma's Mum and Dad rented their own terraced house, her Gran's home was the family hub of activity and fun. No one who knew Gran doubted her love for her four sons, their wives, her grandchildren, the church, and many other waifs and strays.

Gemma stood tearfully waiting for her Gran's departure from the world. She was surrounded by her family in a stark, white room which smelt of bleach and talc in equal measure. Looking at her Gran through tubes and wires and flinching with the faint beep of the heart monitor,

Gemma felt full of fear again. In the final fatal hours her Gran's usual rosy glow had been replaced with a grey, lined complexion. She lay limp and apparently lifeless, suddenly appearing small and fragile in the midst of everyone. Although she was surrounded by family, Gran was clearly a world away from her home on Sandpiper Road. 'This really is it,' thought Gemma. 'How can we all live without our Gran? She has been our rock, our constant, always there for us, never judging, always loving.'

As she watched her Gran's breathing change, a penny dropped in her mind. Gran had something that she wanted. She didn't have the same fresh, excitable faith that Mel and her brother had; it was more mature than that. It was a dependable love that had been there through every situation: unwavering and unending.

Like links in a chain, the family began to take each other's hands around the bed. Emotions were raw and tears began to flow. Everyone knew it was nearly time. Gemma's mouth was dry. She took her brother's hand, suddenly aware of the coldness of hers in his warm comforting palm.

Their vicar was also there and he began to pray. Gemma attentively digested his words: 'Lord, if this is what you want for Gran, if you really want her to be with you, please take her now, so that she will no longer be in pain.'

'Yes, God. Please.' A heavy sense of certainty overcame Gemma as she echoed his prayer in her heart. She was agreeing and believing.

Then her Dad began to pray. Gemma flinched again, but after a few moments, it dawned on her that she was actually enjoying listening to her Dad pray. What had been a boring procedure was now strangely comforting and reassuring. He always spoke earnestly with real feeling, but today there was an added cry of faith in his voice. Gemma couldn't help but observe (perhaps for the first time) that he appeared to have a tangible, authentic relationship with an unseen God.

When he had finished praying they all began to speak out the Lord's Prayer over Gran. She found herself surprisingly recalling every word of it from childhood and quietly mulling over the phrases as they were spoken: '... thy will be done, on earth as it is in heaven.' 'Yes,' she thought, 'your will is better.' For the first time, these words were making sense to Gemma.

As the prayer drew to a close, her uncle leant over the bed and began to sing one of Gran's favourite songs. Gemma would have giggled in the past when a grown man launched into a solo, but not at this moment. As he sang the last line of the song, her uncle lifted his head and tears were streaming uncontrollably down his face.

Gemma quickly looked from him to Gran and instantly knew that she had gone. No longer was her chest rising. No longer was there pain across her face. No longer was Gran in the bleak, clinical room amongst them. Although her body lay in front of them, it just wasn't Gran any more. She was somewhere else. Gemma just knew it in her gut.

Gemma wiped her damp, swollen face, and then hugged each member of her family. As she took one final look at the bed, she noticed that all her fear had gone. She knew that Gran was with God. The longing ache to have her back was superseded by the peace and relief of knowing that Gran was being looked after by her best friend, Jesus.

It felt like the end of an era. Gemma still had to swallow hard when she realized that Sandpiper Road would never again house that warm, joyful greeting. But her mind was overflowing with memories that she could not suppress: Mel's joy the day before the Caesarean; the impossible wonder of holding Sam for the first time; that prayer for her back; and now Gran's emotional (and spiritual) departure. They all played over in her mind like a scratched record.

Gemma began to find herself honestly telling people, 'I'm searching.' Instead of ignoring conversations about God with her family and friends, she had a hunger to hear more. She found it impossible to look at tiny Sam and not think about the bigger picture of life. She was unable to carry on living as if nothing had happened. Gemma wanted what Gran had; she wanted a relationship with God. She wanted the love and the joy. Surely she had to do something about it?

And yet something was still holding her back. She thought about the church, struggling to shake off the embarrassing stereotype that it always conjured up in her mind, and the 'rules' that they would ask her to live by. She wanted the joy, but wouldn't the rest of it cramp her style? And what else would change? Would they judge her for being a teenage mum? What about Jack? What would she have to give up? These weren't Sunday School questions whose answers could be easily found in a colourful paperback. But the very fact that she was asking them made her realize that she no longer dismissed Christianity as a childhood fantasy; it had become a serious option for her life. She felt like she was finally starting to get it. Life is hard. Truth is tough. Faith must be figuring out where they meet.

She could sense that a new chapter was beginning.

2 Ignition

Helen

Helen sat quietly at the rickety old table, never lifting her gaze above the horizontal. It felt as if any attempt to engage her in conversation would result in her bursting into floods of tears. There was a stone wall being presented to anyone who looked, but if anyone had taken the time to look closely at the wall, they would have seen that it was actually a dam. Building up behind it were years of pent-up emotion and frustration that were painfully pushing up against the unmoving façade. Allowing anyone to make even the smallest chip with a chisel-shaped prayer or hug would risk the whole thing splitting right down the middle, creating a disaster-movie-sized cascade that she knew she couldn't control.

Her make-up was failing to bolster these defences. You could see the cracks beginning to appear around her eyes. The shadows within their circumferences spoke more of night than day. Her shoulders formed a fragile sail that would not have caught any prevailing wind.

Helen was just minding her own business without realizing that she was feeling drawn to these strangers. Why else would she be sitting beside them at dinner, when the safer option would have been to stay on her own? It was a night that everyone had been looking forward to for a long time. People from all over this leafy suburb of Leeds had been invited to the church. Folks who had never dared set foot inside a church building had taken that risk for the first time. It was to be a laid-back evening of food, song and chat. But that's not where Helen's head was. It was in another place. Or more accurately, in another time.

Up until a year ago, Helen would have told you that she had a completely normal childhood. This sprang from her gentle nature, that always assumed the best about people, especially her own family. There were always good explanations provided for why things were the way they were. At school she never felt the need to talk about her home life because nobody else did. She didn't really visit her friends' houses because, to be honest, she enjoyed her own company more. She would later reflect that even a few hours in another house might have led her to believe that things at home were not 'normal'. Though she had not realized it, her Dad had suffered from mental health problems for most of his life. Only when the fights between him and her Mum became worryingly regular did her Mum explain what was going on.

As she was approaching thirteen years of age, there was an increased intensity to the fighting that often sent her scurrying in fear to her room. As with so many young people caught up in similar situations, her subconscious coping mechanism was to hide, both physically and psychologically. The foundations of that dam were being built. Any attempt to engage with the situation led to disaster and multiplied fear. When an open bottle of bleach comes flying through the air at you, you think twice about speaking up next time.

But you then also burden yourself with blame for not speaking up more when your Mum can't take any more and suddenly runs away. It had been just another argument about something as trivial as an MOT or an attempt to record a soap opera, but it escalated to the point where the camel's back was broken. Helen didn't know where her Mum had gone.

Helen's brother went to stay with some friends, leaving Helen alone with her Dad. His moods became more and more unstable, and without her Mum acting as a visor, she was experiencing the full force of his illness and rage at first hand. Two days later, her Dad screamed, 'I'm going away to find your mother!' and just left her at home alone. That was bad enough for a fourteen-year-old to cope with, but nothing prepared her for what she found lying on the coffee table the next day.

It was a note addressed to her, written in a scrawl that had obviously become more exasperated as various pens had failed to make a mark on the paper. The top half of the paper looked as if it had been engraved by a sandstorm. Lower down it simply said, 'Sorry Helen, but I can't take any more of this. I won't be coming back. I'm taking my own life.'

'No!' A few seconds of silence. 'No!' A few more seconds of silence. 'No!' she screamed again as she dropped the piece of paper and began to cough and cry uncontrollably. She didn't know what to do, so she simply ran to find her brother. Car horns and squeals from pensioners registered the near misses as she chose the shortest distance between A and B, with her vision and mind obscured by tears and hysteria. When she finally arrived she just cried and cried, holding him like a teddy bear.

Her Dad didn't succeed in ending it all. As with so many in his position, the efficiency of his suicide attempt reflected the rest of his life. Not quite enough alien chemicals got to his liver before the hospital resuscitated him. Helen's Mum had run away to Blackpool, but on hearing what had happened, she returned to Leeds. After a week in hospital he was released, and the first Helen knew of it was when he and her Mum arrived together to pick her up from a school tennis game. Tennis was providing one constant amidst all the variables of her life. This rapprochement didn't last for long, however, as her Dad immediately demanded the car so that he could 'do something important'. When he wouldn't explain why, Helen's Mum refused to hand over the keys, and he pushed her violently to the ground, before driving off. Helen returned home while her Mum was taken to hospital.

Helen had only been through the door five minutes when the phone rang. It was her Dad telling her to leave the line open so that she could listen to him die. By now, this was all far beyond anything that a teenager should have to see or hear. She hung up. He was found by police and readmitted to hospital, but discharged himself. Apparently the hospital should not have let him go. He returned home briefly to tell Helen that he was sorry and then left again. The next day she had to cope with the appalling news that he had hanged himself.

Her memories of these hours were, not surprisingly, cloudy. She wasn't sure that she was even thinking any more. When she wasn't simply numb, she was angry at everyone and everything.

So you can see why a dam becomes an attractive way of managing your inner life. Half of you wants to hide this history from everyone. There's a potent cocktail of shame, ridicule and prejudice to be avoided. But half of you is longing for someone to climb right up to the top of the dam to see the volume of water on the other side. At least then someone else will understand, but the trick is not catching their eye while they're staring down at what they see. Otherwise it's suddenly all too much and all the effort to hold in all that water will be wasted. One person she definitely wasn't letting over that wall was God. She didn't want to know about him. In fact, she hated him for taking her Dad away in the cruellest of ways.

Those horrendous moments were now a whole year away, but eating dinner beside this girl, none of these strangers knew why she was hiding while in full view. At that point she didn't know that these girls were part of a Youth For Christ band that would be performing that night, but something about them seemed warm and open. They had a light in their eyes that she thought she had had once and would love to have again. Their questions to her were innocent and expectant of good things. Communicating nothing of note was better than disappointing them.

That small connection meant that when they played their songs later, she was listening with every fibre of her being. But it wasn't easy. She knew in her gut that there was a battle going on that night. The band members spent much of the evening praying backstage, as they also felt that they were in the midst of a spiritual fight for the souls of those in the room. There was a lot of disturbance and distraction in the hall from rowdy teenagers, and some of those who left the hall released their clockwork-like tension by smashing windows in the pub across the road.

The presence of police hovering at the back of a venue is never the most encouraging sight for a band or a preacher to see.

Towards the end of the evening, the band sang a song that spoke about the love of God the Father reaching out to his prodigal sons and daughters. The fact that this love was being offered to the biblical prodigal son, no matter where he had been and no matter what he had been doing, blew Helen away. God was constant. The idea of a stable, loving father was not something she had ever thought about. It was hard to imagine a father whose mood could be depended on from one moment to the next. She had been let down and betrayed by the only man that she had called Dad, so could this love be for real?

She started to wonder if this love had in fact been with her in the past year. She remembered all those 'coincidences' when people had appeared just as she was about to try to kill herself again. She remembered feeling hugged by something. Right now, she could feel arms of love wrapped right around her, but what really finished her off was realizing that they had been there all along. The dam broke. There were floods of pain, joy, anger and love all streaming together from inside to outside. It was confusing and wonderful all at the same time. She sang along with the band, 'Into your open arms I throw myself'. That was a level of freedom and vulnerability she hadn't known in a long time. In 'honeymoon mode', she excitedly emailed the girls from the band to let them know what had happened, without divulging much information about her story.

A few months later, she was baptized and dived into the activities of the local church, but after a while the enormity of what had happened in her family began to press down on her again. She became depressed, and struggled to let go of it all. Helen couldn't understand why all this was happening, and she channelled her frustration through punching walls and other objects. Over a period of time, she started to inflict serious damage on herself but never told anyone about it.

Fast forward nine months to the summer of 2006. Not much had changed. Helen was at a large Christian event called Soul Survivor. She was desperate to simply feel happy, but in her own words, 'God had other plans'. Halfway through the week, during one of the evening meetings, there was an invitation given from the stage that Helen knew she should respond to. Anyone who was finding it hard to forgive was asked to come down to the front of the gathering. Helen went down to the front planning to forgive the hospital staff for letting her Dad out, but when she arrived there, she realized that she needed to do what had always been too painful to do – actually to forgive her Dad. Again in her own words, 'God pinned me down until I forgave my Dad for all that he had put me through.' It was a time of real trauma but also real release, as the reality of the impact of all his actions and inaction landed on her. She hadn't even known that she was so angry with him, but by the end of it she was filled with an awesome peace that left her smiling from ear to ear.

She also felt God telling her to share this peace with other people, and as she was asking 'Who?', three people laid their hands on her. Her back began to burn at the position of their hands, and she asked God to look after them and help sort out their problems. None of them knew each other, and as they shared their stories they discovered each of them had suffered the loss of an unborn child, whether as a parent or a sibling. They reported that they had experienced a sense of that hurt being healed when they were praying with Helen.

She was astounded. But more was to come. Later that night another boy was praying and called Helen's name out. She went over and held his hand and prayed healing over him. He had suffered for years from ring-worm scars and they simply disappeared as she prayed. This second shock caused Helen to fall down and just revel in God's presence for about an hour.

She marvelled at the fact that God had used a wounded, broken human being as a healer. The dam had been replaced by a stream of fresh water that was already refreshing other people.

The next day she emailed her old dining companions again. This time they heard the whole story.

3 Acceleration

Tim

Have you ever been stuck with a bunch of strangers in a confined space for an uncomfortable length of time? A broken lift? A delayed plane, perhaps? If we discount recovering 'reality TV' participants, then the answer is probably not many of us! We tend to avoid that type of situation in life. In fact, we go out of our way to keep our personal space private, foolishly thinking that they are one and the same thing. This is never more so than when we use public transport. Is it fear, suspicion or simple laziness that prevents us from interacting with those around us? Do we become less of who we truly are? Are we neutered by our surroundings? Are our magazines, iPods, novels, newspapers and laptops merely colourful 'Do not disturb' signs for our souls? Anything for a quiet life. This awkwardness-evasion leaves us challenge-free and comfortable.

It had been a long, tiring weekend for both of them, so Tim and Steve had every reason to be 'keeping themselves to themselves'. Tim had always wondered about that phrase. He thought it was funny that the only time you ever heard it on TV was when the truth about someone's real character emerged. You heard it from neighbours when it turned out that Mr Johnson from number 47 was actually a conspirator in a plot to bomb an embassy, or that Mr Stephens from number 24 was having his hard drives removed for police scrutiny. 'You wouldn't believe it – he always kept himself to himself.' It's stated as if it is a noble, positive characteristic, elevated to the status of something you could put on your CV. Tim, however, knew from grim experience that 'keeping himself to himself' was a major contributing factor in the development of such unhealthy behaviour patterns, undeterred by the normal checks and balances of family and community life.

Ironically, these two lads had been sharing an experience that was intensely personal, but which they could not keep private. Having never had any previous connection with church or God, they had both recently met someone called Jesus. They were both experiencing the excitement and intensity of doing 'gap years' with Youth For Christ, sharing their stories and lives with other young people in schools, streets and churches.

Tonight they were on the 17:30 from Middlesbrough to Newcastle. Tim was the sort of 'youth' who would alert your 'awkward' sensors and might actually cause you to move to the next carriage. If you were judging only by appearances, you would suspect that he was the harbinger of much hassle. He sat with his chin jutting out confidently and his pierced ear parading his individuality for all to see. This was in contrast to the insecure stubble that was tentatively populating the lower half of his face. His head had been shaved by an electric razor using the setting somewhere between 'disagreeable' and 'aggressive'. His jacket had become, to all intents and purposes, a handbag, though he would never admit to that. It was weighed down by cash, keys, a mobile phone, and another item that he felt sure would surprise anyone who had jumped to any conclusions about him – a Bible.

If they had met him a year earlier, their suspicions would have been better founded. Tim left home aged seventeen, and bounced around various towns, experimenting with every type of illicit substance he could find. In his own words he was 'super-selfish' – living for himself, by himself, only making friends with someone to make it easier to steal their iPod a week later. He would try absolutely anything, his only stipulation being that it should alter his mental state – so alcohol, speed, ecstasy, or the contents of medicine cabinets were his regular ports of call. He never cared about the consequences of his actions, which often left him homeless for prolonged periods.

It had been a strange December day. Tim wasn't meant to be on this train. He had planned to simply meet Steve at the gig in Newcastle. But for some reason he'd experienced what he could only describe as a gut urge to hook up with him earlier in Middlesbrough. However, he arrived there at the start of the afternoon to find that Steve was still at work. Forward planning still wasn't a strong point for him. Cue four hours of wandering around Middlesbrough questioning his gut instincts. The end result of all this was his presence on the 17:30 with a perplexed Steve by his side.

About an hour into their journey, a couple of miles north of Sunderland, there was a crescendo of screaming brakes. It was as if the driver had been asked to perform an emergency stop. The panic-stricken passengers braced themselves for an impact, digging nails into the tatty seats. None came. The deceleration from sixty miles per hour to zero in the space of a few seconds caused a simultaneous, communal intake of breath. Squawks and screams were followed by sighs of relief as people realized that their limbs were all still where they should be. But this was followed by a fraught period – that felt like five hours but probably only lasted thirty seconds – during which people were both physically and psychologically preparing themselves for what would come next. Was another train hurtling towards them? Was this a terrorist attack? Had they hit something?

The train comprised only two carriages and the lads were sitting right in the middle of the front carriage. Initial panic was channelled into discussion. Could a tree have come down on the track? The weather hadn't been that bad. Was it just another signalling error?

If you had asked Tim to give you five words that would best describe him, you would have got these: impulsive, outgoing, confident, passionate and up-front. No one else in the carriage was moving, so he went straight up to the front to see what was going on. Since he had become a Christian these traits, that had once got him into so much trouble, had enabled him to have a significant impact on most people he met. He had experienced a shocking reversal from wanting to steal from people, to actively trying to give to them. But nothing had prepared him for what he would experience as he pulled open the door into the driver's compartment.

A pale, middle-aged man was shaking in his seat. His eyelids were uncomfortably performing the splits, as he stared into space, unblinking. 'I think I've killed her. I think I've killed her. I think...' Also present was a conductor who was attempting to calm him down. The driver didn't even acknowledge Tim's presence.

'Are you OK?' Tim asked. 'What's happened?'

'I think we may have had a fatality', the conductor replied, but before Tim could ask any more, the conductor dismissed him.

Tim could feel every eye on him as he stepped back into the carriage. He experienced what every politician conducting a press conference must experience when confronted by a rush of questions leapfrogging one another. None of them were questions he could answer. 'How long will we be delayed for? I need to be in Newcastle in twenty minutes for a meeting. Am I going to get there?'

The innate selfishness of the questions annoyed Tim, but he did his best to calm everyone down before discovering that he was, in fact, capable of spin: 'There's no need for alarm, but there is a small chance that we may have hit someone.' Their questions stayed selfish, and he wondered if they had actually heard what he had said.

The conductor seemed well out of his depth in a crisis situation and wouldn't let anyone get off the train. Was there even anyone outside checking what was going on? 'Emergency services have been informed' was all that they were told.

Tim went back to his seat beside Steve and explained what he had seen. Steve's first response was to start praying and Tim joined him. In the mayhem of the unknown, two heads were bowed. They prayed for whoever had been hit. They prayed for the driver and the conductor – for calm heads in a difficult situation, and especially that the driver wouldn't carry around any guilt from what had happened. They also prayed for all the other passengers so that there would be an atmosphere of peace on the train. Across the aisle from the lads sat a mixed-race guy with the word 'Gangsta' emblazoned across his jacket. His mobile conversations and his extensive bling hadn't been doing anything to dissuade the lads from drawing the conclusion that he was labelled appropriately. While they were praying he leant over and prodded Tim, asking, 'What you doing?' Tim's instant reply was something he later laughed about – 'I can't talk right now, mate, we're praying.' The man's flowery vocabulary was suddenly reduced to 'Oh!'

When the boys came up for air, they found out that this guy's name was Julian and that he was genuinely interested in what they'd been doing. Tim explained, 'We need God to help in this situation. We're friends of God.' He explained a little bit more about prayer but was getting that bottom-lip-protruding look from Julian.

Just then the conductor popped out to confirm that a girl had definitely been hit by the train and that there would be a short delay as they waited for an ambulance team and the transport police.

The reality was dawning on Tim and Steve that it wasn't an accident that they'd got this train together. They'd had these adventures together before. They reminisced about the time they had used the intercom of a plane cabin to preach to their fellow passengers. Their current prayers became more creative, asking for angelic protection for those connected with the accident, and grace over any situations that were being caused by the train's lateness.

The conductor then confirmed that they would be stuck there for at least another hour, which led to large-scale recriminations from the other passengers. Questions were asked about compensation and taxis.

Tim was amazed at how the only common language that these strangers seemed to be able to share was 'moaning'.

Tim and Steve wanted to go outside to attempt to help or pray for the girl who had been hit, but the conductor vigorously prevented them. They felt that he was stalling for the police, when urgent action was really required. (It later became clear that the conductor was simply trying to prevent anyone else having to see what he had seen on stepping down on to the track.)

After a while the tension in the carriage dissipated as everyone had sent their texts and made their calls of explanation. Folks were now just sitting and processing in the privacy of their own heads. The boys' praying had surprised and confused everyone else in the carriage. Their 'yoofish' looks belied what was going on below the surface. People would later report that they couldn't believe how calm the boys had been in the midst of the crisis. Even though the boys didn't pray for themselves, they just knew that God had filled them with his Holy Spirit.

Julian piped up again: 'Where were you guys going, anyway?' When he found out that they were missing a concert that they had already paid for, he was confused by their calmness. 'Are youze not super cheesed off?' Tim startled him even more when he admitted that he was actually excited at the thought of being stuck with this many people for three whole hours, as it gave him the opportunity to tell them about Jesus. He had a captive audience!

As their conversation progressed Tim and Julian realized that they had a lot in common. They were both keen amateur DJs and shared a passion for the same hip-hop acts. Tim could also identify with Julian's drug-riddled lifestyle, and Julian couldn't believe that this Christian

36

knew all the lingo from in and around the drug scene. He sat open-mouthed as Tim explained how Jesus had changed him.

Another common point of their history was that they would spend most evenings drunk. Julian reached into his rucksack to get his usual 'packed lunch' of a Special Brew four-pack to help the hours go faster. To his horror, they weren't there. He complained, 'I pack four every day – they're the only thing I have to look forward to at the end of the day.'

'Maybe it's no coincidence that you forgot them today,' said Tim. 'Maybe you need to be sober to hear what I have to say,' he added cheekily. Tim levelled with Julian, asking him to imagine lying in a field on a summer afternoon having a spliff.

Julian threw back a knowing smile. 'Easy,' he replied.

'So take it from someone who knows,' Tim continued. 'Being with God is ten times better than that.'

What Julian found harder to believe was that even though Tim was well aware of the 'positive' effects of the drug, he was saying that he would never smoke weed again. He said he wouldn't gamble with it, as it could jeopardize his relationship with God.

In response, Julian shared with Tim about how he didn't look forward to going home because of his brother's steroid-abusing rage and his parents' explosive relationship.

Tim didn't have to squeeze God into the conversation. It was simply obvious to mention him. It felt utterly natural. He had never felt that Christianity was so real or relevant.

Their lengthy conversation was attracting the attention of others in the carriage. Some were openly listening while others were giving away their interest with correctly timed laughter from behind their magazines. It was the only show in town.

Taking particular interest was a guy called Pabon who was from Bangladesh. At one point he volunteered his own story. 'I'm a Hindu and I'm not sure I believe what you're saying.'

Steve replied, 'So what do you believe?' A verbal tennis match ensued, with both of them reading portions out of Tim's Bible and challenging each other's assumptions and assertions. The heads of those watching twisted from side to side like eager spectators in Centre Court. This infectious freedom of expression was breaking people out of their private little travelling worlds. In their souls, this counter-cultural openness was something that they wanted, but in reality found it hard to express. It was certainly a freeing experience for Pabon to question what had always been unquestionable. His faith was very much inherited, whereas Tim and Steve had found theirs for themselves. The communication was all good-natured and the chat was spattered with enough good one-liners to allow the onlookers to relax enough to keep listening.

Into the midst of this positive experience arrived a party of four girls from a few seats away who had been using the spare time to get progressively more drunk. They weren't happy that their party was being upset by civil discussion. 'What are you doing?' 'What are you talking about?' they screamed. They all had scraggy, bleach blonde hair and were dressed to undress.

The boys replied, 'We were just talking about Jesus. Do you want to listen?'

They responded by simply mocking the lads, on subjects as wide-ranging as the boys' zits and masturbation. 'If you're made in the image

38

of God, then why is he so ugly?' they said, pointing at another, younger lad. Their attacks were so personal and vindictive that even the sternest atheist in the carriage would have been hoping that they would be quiet. Quickly.

They seemed to cover every controversial question, from suffering to sexuality. The boys suppressed the temptation to verbally take them to pieces (as it would have been easy to do). 'Look at the state of you lot – you've obviously got life down,' is what Tim would have loved to say. Instead they kept a respectful silence when necessary and, at other times, calmly answered as well as they could, before the subject was hijacked by another tangent. The boys felt that this circumstance had been engineered by the devil as an attempt to derail what had been going on.

When the girls finally walked off, the boys felt an overwhelming sense of victory, and a couple of onlookers reached out to shake their hands, saying things like, 'Well played. That was out of order.' It felt as if they had turned the situation around into an opportunity to practise what they had just been preaching.

Over the next few minutes, the conversation with Pabon became very intense as he explained about the different Hindu gods and Steve encouraged him to read about Jesus for himself. So folks barely noticed that the police and ambulance crew had arrived and were dealing with what had happened. The victim was a sixteen-year-old girl who had been drinking at the top of a railway siding. She had tripped and stumbled downwards onto the track in front of the oncoming train. She had died instantly.

The occupants of the train were shocked and silent on hearing the tragic news. After some moments of silence, there were affirming hugs and glances all round. The inevitable community that is constructed in times of crisis was given expression.

As the train started to move again, Pabon shared more of his story. He felt a heavy burden to provide for his family back in Bangladesh, and racist undercurrents left him feeling distinctly uncomfortable in the area where he lived. Crime was a constant fear. Julian had been listening with increasing interest to Pabon's description of his neighbourhood, and chipped in, 'What street do you live on, my man?' Unbelievably, they lived on the same street. Julian offered to be his 'big brother' and look after him. As they got off at the next stop together, Julian threw an affectionate arm around him. (And he hadn't been smoking anything!)

'What a result!' thought Tim and Steve. They were left thinking about Pabon's last words before he got off the train: 'Thank you for challenging me. It has really got me thinking about what I do believe. Perhaps I will read more of the Bible.'

The boys were staring into space, amazed at what had just happened. It was time to pray again – this time to say thanks. Tim had never felt more satisfied in his life. He was doing what he had been put on the planet to do. In his own words, 'At those times, I could get shot and not feel it.' Both inside and outside that carriage, issues of life and death were played out by the young people of Britain. In the midst of the tragedy and the headlines, real young people had made a real difference in each other's lives.

A few weeks later, on New Year's Eve, Tim got a phone call that he hadn't expected. Steve called to explain that he had just been walking through Newcastle City Centre and had heard a vaguely familiar voice calling his name. He turned sideways to see the shy little figure of Pabon running towards him with the biggest smile on his face. He grabbed

Steve's right hand with both his hands and shook it like a cocktail shaker. 'Steve, I went away and did some research. I've been seeking the truth, and I've found what I'm looking for. It's Jesus. I've given my life to him. I'm a Christian!'

There was a life and energy about him that he just hadn't had that night on the train. He had to run on quickly to meet someone, but there was time enough for him to say that he was 'working on Julian – it's only a matter of time', and to again thank Steve for being brave enough to tell him the truth.

Steve was so blown away that, as Pabon ran off, all he could think of to shout after him was 'Happy New Year!' – but those words had never felt more appropriate.

The Name's Peter – Simon Peter

Let me introduce you to another disciple. This one is called Simon, except he's also called Peter. To avoid confusion with the other Simons, he tends to get called Simon Peter. That sounds a bit too much like a children's TV programme for my liking, but at least he's one of the first people who can lay claim to having a 'Christian' name. Not many other folks can blame the man himself!

As far as we can tell from ancient writings, Simon Peter was an average bloke. He was tall, but not very tall. Trim, but not thin. Like me, he was a Factor 45 kid (though I guess they didn't have sun cream in those days), with folks reporting a very pale complexion as the backdrop for a short, tightly curled beard.

He was born in the town of Bethsaida, in the province of Galilee. The Sea of Galilee (actually a lake) was the heartbeat of the region, and Simon Peter's father Jonah was in fact a fisherman. Simon Peter and his brother Andrew went into business with James and John, who were the sons of another fisherman called Zebedee. To underline the fact that we are talking about a real human being, as real as the young people in this book, you can still visit the house in which Simon Peter lived. In fact I have. It's in Capernaum, just a bit further round the Galilean coast. However, if you go to visit, don't expect a cup of tea. The Christians of the fifth century helpfully built a church on top of it.

Roller coaster of emotion

If I had to pick one figure in the public eye who has a bit of the Simon Peter about him, it would have to be the England cricketer Andrew 'Freddie' Flintoff. Like Simon Peter, he's whole-hearted, boisterous, honest about his mistakes and utterly committed to his cause. So it's not surprising that Freddie's stock phrase during media interviews at the end of the summer of 2005 sums up the life of Mr Peter (or Simon to you and me). Let me explain.

I felt like a bit of an oddity in Trafalgar Square – an Irishman screaming his guts out for the England cricket team. The thousands present were overjoyed that England had miraculously won back the Ashes from Australia. But there was one man whom the crowd were waiting to see above all the others. Our Freddie. When he appeared to a tumultuous reception, it was obvious even to those standing hundreds of yards away that Freddie had enjoyed a long night. In fact I think he still thought it was yesterday. His words were slurred and his eyes (appropriately enough) resembled two cricket balls. With his fragile grasp on reality, he was falling back on one stock phrase when asked any question by any interviewer. I had already heard him use it twice that day, both on radio and on television. By the end of the day some eagle-eared journalist had counted twenty-seven uses of the phrase by Freddie in his various public appearances.

'So, how does it feel to have won the Ashes, Freddie?'

'Well, Mark [or insert another name as appropriate], it's been a roller coaster of emotion! You know, the whole summer has been one big roller coaster of emotion!' There it is. Again. The interviewer hadn't even asked another question yet.

Simon Peter's life was quite literally 'a roller coaster of emotion'. From the highs of adrenaline-soaked moments like the Transfiguration to the gut-wrenching lows of his famous betrayal or any of Jesus' verbal rebukes, Simon Peter experienced every emotion possible on his journey with Jesus. He is the follower of Jesus whom we know most about – there are over 200 mentions of him in the New Testament, which is streets ahead of any of the other disciples. Yet somehow we believe that we are made of different DNA to Peter. We believe that we are more sophisticated and immune to the ups and downs of life that Peter experienced. Surely our expectations and hopes would be a lot healthier if, every so often on our journey with Jesus, we were to sneak a glance over our shoulder and catch the eye of a bearded fisherman, who is winking back at us, letting us know that he's been there too.

Like Tim in the last chapter, I've realized that so many of the young people we have the privilege of working with in Youth For Christ have striking similarities to Peter. Many will never go near third-level education. Many come from families with no religious heritage. Many start with no experience of speaking in public and little knowledge of scripture. But the biggest similarity is that many of them are with us because someone has taken a risk with them. Someone has spotted their potential in the midst of their confusion and wayward behaviour, and has called out their true selves. They are often like Peter – promising failures. It has been my privilege to be part of an organization where there is a culture of risk-taking – often with those whom no one else would dare take a risk with. But in doing this, I believe we are stepping into the shoes of a man from Galilee who put his faith in twelve men who had gold buried in their dust. The secret was that he had the patience to sift through and find it. Gemma, Helen, Amy, Rebecca, Shaun, Jemima, Lewis, Brian, Anthony, Tim and Evan are disciples who follow that same man.

Part of the problem, or part of the solution?

We live in an age where young people are being labelled as a problem to which we need solutions. As a young person reading some of our daily newspapers, you could be forgiven for thinking that adult society would simply rather do without you. A politician telling you to show more respect would probably make you wince at the irony, if he was actually speaking a language you could understand. Before anyone throws stones on subjects like respect, we need to stop for a moment, preferably somewhere near a mirror. If young people have got a problem in this area, where have they learnt it from? We were products of the generation before us and were quick to blame them for various attitudes or circumstances that we inherited.

Visit any of our sixty-five Youth For Christ centres and, from the Isle of Wight to the Shetlands, from Norfolk to Devon, you will find the same thing. You will find something that isn't being reported in the media. You will find young people showing bucket-loads of respect to the generation above them because they feel as if they are being listened to by that generation. Respect breeds respect. I will never forget receiving a letter from a young guy who had just spent a week with a Youth For Christ team. He wrote, 'For the first time in my life, I heard about God in a way that I could understand, from people that I could understand.'

There is no magic formula involved. On your trip, you would simply meet people (aged sixteen to eighty!) who *believe* in young people, meeting them where they're at, geographically, psychologically and spiritually. Often young people are being engaged creatively through music, dance, rap or theatre workshops, giving expression to their frustrations, joys and confusion. When you dig below the surface with young people and listen to their stories, you will start to understand the environmental factors that shape their lives. You start to understand someone's constant attention-grabbing behaviour when you realize that she's never had the attention of an older male in her life. You start to understand his constant fighting when you realize that he's never been shown any other way of resolving a conflict.

But there is good news. There is a generation of young people who don't care what is written about them, and they are rising up to make an impact on their friends, neighbourhoods and nation. They don't make the news, because the positive impact they are having is neither scandalous nor tragic, and somehow those words have come to define what is newsworthy in the Western world. So don't expect to hear about these young people on your TV or in your glossy magazines, but keep your ear to the ground. All over the UK, young people are coming together to serve their communities in the name of Jesus, bringing his love through word and deed. That's good news.

What's in a name?

The simple answer is 'an awful lot'. For those of us who have been the subjects of name-based playground bullying, we need no reminding of that. From the ages of six to fourteen I drank my tea or milk every morning from a mug that bore my name. ANDREW. The verse began:

> You give life your all
> And go the whole length.
> You're truly resilient
> With great inner strength.
> On every occasion you...

From there it starts to get fuzzy, but I'm constantly amazed by the fact that I can still quote those first four lines verbatim. I've begun to suspect that those words, which I read at breakfast-time every day, have actually spoken something very powerful into my life. I remember those lines bouncing around my head at random moments, and I'd like to think that to some extent I've been able to live them out. Imagine if those four lines had been:

> You sit on the fence,
> And struggle to spell.
> You fear other people
> Who don't wish you well...

I wonder if my life would have turned out differently! In his book *Freakonomics*, Steven D. Levitt explains that there is a statistically proven aspirant tendency when parents name their children. They are always calling their children upwards to stretch beyond their present station. The names used by parents who are rich, famous and successful are the names that filter down to those who dream of that for their children and themselves. The flow never goes in the other direction.

Another Andrew (who probably didn't have a mug) facilitated the moment where Simon was given a new name. It was the day after Jesus had been baptized in the Jordan. Simon's brother Andrew is a disciple of John the Baptist, but as you can see from verse 37, he needed no invitation to become a disciple of someone else.

> The next day John was there again with two of his disciples. When he saw Jesus passing by, he said, 'Look, the Lamb of God!'
>
> When the two disciples heard him say this, they followed Jesus. Turning round, Jesus saw them following and asked, 'What do you want?'
>
> They said, 'Rabbi' (which means Teacher), 'where are you staying?'
>
> 'Come,' he replied, 'and you will see.'
>
> So they went and saw where he was staying, and spent that day with him. It was about the tenth hour.
>
> Andrew, Simon Peter's brother, was one of the two who heard what John had said and who had followed Jesus. The first thing Andrew did was to find his brother Simon and tell him, 'We have found the Messiah' (that is, the Christ). And he brought him to Jesus.
>
> Jesus looked at him and said, 'You are Simon son of John. You will be called Cephas' (which, when translated, is Peter).   (John 1:35–42)

That is a pretty bold thing to do on first contact with someone. Usually a nickname is an indicator of a shared period of intimacy. It's a label that lets you know that you belong, but you only expect it after the ice has been broken and people have begun to know and understand you.

However, the piece of this puzzle that we may have missed while discussing what Simon's new name actually meant is the start of the sentence: 'Jesus looked at him...' In a wonderful but chilling resonance, the Greek word used here, *emblepo*, is the same word used in Luke 22:61 in an altogether different situation. At that point it describes the piercing gaze of Jesus across Caiaphas' courtyard after Peter's denials. When Jesus looks at you, you know you've been looked at. He doesn't merely glance, or catch your eye. He looks at you. He sees you. He sees the real you. He sees not only what you are but what you can be. He sees the treasure in the dust of a life that hasn't been tidied up in a while. In the midst of a world that goes digging for dirt, he actively goes digging for gold. He sees the rainbow in the rain of our stormy lives.

For I believe he looks and sees something of himself in us. Some of the most precious moments of my life have occurred when I have seen traits and actions in others that I recognize in myself. When these are positive traits, it's all the better! There is something incredibly special about seeing something in someone that reveals that they see the world the way you do, when you'd previously thought no one else saw it that way. How wonderful it is that God looks us in the eye and sees something of himself. I almost cannot believe that I carry the DNA of the Holy Creator of the universe. And that is part of the problem.

Image

I fear we have allowed circumstances to shape our theology, rather than the other way round. The Bible makes it perfectly clear that every single human being is made in the image of God:

Then God said, 'Let us make man in our image, in our likeness, and let them rule over the fish of the sea and the birds of the air, over the livestock, over all the earth, and over all the creatures that move along the ground.'

So God created man
in his own image,
in the image of God
he created him;
male and female
he created them.
(Genesis 1:26–27)

We have often become so caught up in the discussion of gender when looking at these verses that we fail to see the glorious truth blazing out from the page. We are made in the image of God. Do you remember O-level or GCSE physics? An image is a two-dimensional, touchable, accessible representation of a three-dimensional object. Think of a flat movie screen representing 3-D action, or the white disc you can produce via a lens on a page representing the sun. Can you believe that that big uncontrollable ball of flaming gas can be reduced to a minute little white disc? Amazing. And that dropping down of a dimension is even more phenomenal when you realize that we are carriers of the image of God! How can all that beauty and glory be represented by a pesky little human being?

Only one human ever represented that glory perfectly. This is how Paul described Jesus:

He is the image of the invisible God, the firstborn over all creation.
(Colossians 1:15)

The Greek word *eikon* used here denotes an exact image drawn from the same material as the original, as opposed to simply being a likeness, which merely resembles it. Jesus was the perfect human being. The perfect carrier of the image of God. The important thing to note is that it didn't make him any less human, it actually made him more human. Humanity is perfected when we fully display God's image. But we've stopped believing we can carry it because we've stopped believing that Jesus was human. The first disciples knew that he was human. They walked and talked with him. They struggled to grab onto the fact that he was divine. We have the opposite problem. We know he was divine, but we have stopped believing he was just like us. He slept, he shopped, he ate and he digested. I won't go any further!

So if it's hard to believe that we are carriers of the image of God, how much harder is it to believe that someone else is, especially when their behaviour annoys us intensely? I fear that we've stopped believing that every young person we meet is a carrier of the image of God. Granted, that image may be blurred, broken or shattered by bad decisions, or circumstances that perhaps they have had no control over, but it is still there. It is too easy in this day and age to write people off, before they have even been given a chance.

Inside every young person is the essence of their creator, however buried it may be. It has been my privilege, through working with Youth For Christ, to see that image restored in so many young lives, often through the kindling of what was already there, but which no one else had noticed.

Behind bars

This holds true even in the extreme scenarios of Young Offenders' institutions. I will never forget my first morning at Castington Prison. About fifteen lads paraded in with the classic 'hard' exterior, keen to let me know that I was on their turf, and that we would be playing by their rules! We were encouraging them to take part in a rap-writing workshop. At the end of the week they would perform the rap that they had written to the other inmates. Carefully placed verbal darts came my way for the first few minutes as they jockeyed for position with the new boy. Then I was met with looks of utter disbelief as they realized that this strange Irish guy was actually suggesting that they could create something worthwhile and that someone else would listen to it! The beginning of the process was as hard as getting blood out of a stone, and then transfusing it into some bodies close to death!

I encouraged the lads to be brutally honest about how they were feeling. They had a chance to vent all their frustrations at 'the system'. It quite literally was 'rage against the machine'. That rage is usually being directed at other inmates, wardens and walls. Their first drafts painted a dark but honest picture of the inside of their cells and, more importantly, the inside of their heads and hearts. I suggested that instead of expressing their annoyance at some generic 'system' which seemed more like a nebulous fog, why not express their annoyance to someone who would actually be listening and might actually respond? Why not address these words to God? They were surprised that I wanted to expose God to that sort of verbal battery. 'Don't worry,' I said, 'he's big enough to handle himself.'

Half an hour later the lads came back, and the change in dynamic was palpable. Something had happened. It was all still very angry and honest, and the lyrics wouldn't be suitable for printing here, but there was an added reflection in the tone and content that hadn't been there before.

After the first lad finished, I said, 'Well done, mate – you've just written your first Psalm.'

'What? No way – no, I haven't – no!' he blurted as he stepped back in surprise. I went on to read some of David's angrier work from the Bible, and they started to see what I meant, nodding their heads in agreement.

By getting creative they were connecting with their creator. They were exercising the creative spark placed in them by the one in whose image they were made. An inevitable connection to God is made when you do that. A link is forged (even if it's only subconscious) when a child does something that they have seen their parents doing. And in the prison, not only was that creative connection occurring, they were actually communicating with God. Whether they liked it or not, they were praying. It may have been a modest start, but a real relationship was beginning. A relationship based on honest communication. We all know that those are the relationships that last, rather than the ones where we're pretending, simply saying all the right things at the right time. How will we ever know where young people are at if we only let them sing the words we tell them to sing, or say the words we tell them to say?

Time and time again we have seen these first creative moments in music, dance or art – the little baby steps at the start of a journey of faith. A connection is made, and in the right supportive environment, many of these young people, including the lads in prison, have become Christians.

ID cards

So if you truly believe that every human being you interact with is a carrier of the image of God, does that not change how you interact with them? To quote Vinoth Ramachandrara, when you stand face to face with another human being, you are standing in the presence of 'a vehicle of the divine'. Does that affect how you treat the cleaner at your school, or the young person hunched on your street corner, or the guy behind the counter at McDonalds, or the lady working in the call centre?

Try an experiment for me. Keep a postcard in your pocket (you could call it an ID card!). On it make an attempt to note down what you see of the image of God in every person that you meet in the next twenty-four hours (especially the young people). It may be their gentle smile; it may be their perseverance with an ailing relative; it may be their sporting prowess. Write these things down. The day I spent doing this changed the way I look at people for ever. It shamed me. I can be so quick to criticize and so slow to spot goodness.

Through the fall, the image of God has been blurred, broken and distorted, but not lost altogether. When I look at young people whose lives have been upset from the start by dysfunctional family scenarios, but who have compounded it by making some crazy decisions, I feel the immense pain of it and I struggle to come up with a way of describing what is going on. What follows is the closest I've come to doing it.

Pieces

Imagine that the image of God is represented by the photograph on the top of a jigsaw-puzzle box. But rather than the box being calmly set down on a coffee table, and the pieces lifted out, it's as if someone has simply tipped all the pieces out over the floor and thrown away the box. This is what so many young people's home lives feel like – young people like Helen. The image is still there but it's in pieces and they feel in their guts that these pieces should go together somehow, but someone has taken away their box. Someone has taken away the big picture that explains how all the fragments of a life can make sense together. This leads to a desperate groping around for the missing big picture, and frantic attempts to put their pieces together in whatever way seems to look right. The twisted thing that results just adds to the frustration. The attempts to make it work often take the image further away from what it was meant to be.

It feels like what we've been doing for young people with Youth For Christ is explaining the big story and giving them back the box. They start to see that their life has innate value because they are uniquely created in love. The lyrics of this TVB song say it well:

No one else could ever think like you
No one else could play your part
No one else could do the things you do
You're custom-made right from the start.

Knowing your value, and more importantly, where it comes from, conveys a sense of purpose which frees young people from desperately seeking meaning and purpose from their achievements. Once people can understand their lives in the context of the big story of God, it's amazing how the ultimate Healer puts the broken pieces back together again.

Eyes on the future

Can we look at someone else (or ourselves, for that matter) and see the future, rather than the present or past? Can we see what could be, rather than what is? That's what Jesus did with Simon. Simon was the present and past. Peter was the future. John 2:25 says it brilliantly:

He did not need man's testimony about man, for he knew what was in a man.

It's also what will happen in the stories of Lewis and Brian, later in the book. It takes a trained eye to see the unseen. To see real potential. The first person who tried to make a phone work without a lead attached was probably ridiculed. But no more than twenty years later, you can lay out the world's mobiles end to end all the way to the moon. Or can you imagine the first committee meeting where someone said, 'I've had an idea. Right at the heart of some of the most famous, ancient, beautiful architecture in the world, let's build a massive Ferris wheel! In fact, let's make it so big that it dwarfs all the other buildings!' I suspect that not everyone was convinced. But again, ten years later, the London Eye is one of the most popular tourist attractions in the world. Do we have our eyes wide enough open to see people's potential?

Peter means 'rock'. So this isn't a new name for the sake of it, simply marking a change of lifestyle. It's a prophetic calling out of the real Simon Peter, who will become the 'rock on which I build my church' (Matthew 16:18). The most important word in that last statement may well be 'I'. Often we don't trust young people with roles because we've begun to believe that they or we do the building, rather than Jesus. This is one foreman whom we can trust to stay on the job and get it right.

We often only reflect on the religious leaders' opinion of the disciples as it reflects on their opinion of Jesus. But is there a Pharisaical aspect to how we look at young people, wishing that they had a theology degree before they lead a small group or preach a sermon? The key question is, do we really want young people to become more like Jesus, or more like us? One will make us feel more comfortable, and the other will make us feel less comfortable. One will enable us to feel good about our way of life, and the other will challenge it.

I would love to know what was going on in Simon Peter's mind and heart after hearing his new name. Is he thinking that this bloke has some cheek? Is he liking the tough-sounding 'Rocky'? Has he any clue about the size of the building that will be planted on that rock? To us it sounds vaguely normal to have the name Peter, but it wasn't in use as a name until the third century AD, so Jesus really was actually calling him 'Rock'. It's not a nickname – it's a state-ment of intent. It would be like you or I being called 'Brick' (but I don't think that will ever catch on). In normal conversation, Jesus still called Peter Simon.

The problem with so much of the potential in young people, even when it has actually been recognized and spoken out, is that without the right environ-ment for its development, it can dissipate so quickly. Peter has the privilege of spending his days with the best small-group leader of all time. He is planted in very fertile ground. The challenge for us is whether or not we can help form that fertile environment for the incubation of the potential in the young people who journey with us. Let's learn about how Jesus did that as Simon Peter's journey unfolds in Matthew's Gospel.

Cod calling

> As Jesus was walking beside the Sea of Galilee, he saw two brothers, Simon called Peter and his brother Andrew. They were casting a net into the lake, for they were fishermen. 'Come, follow me,' Jesus said, 'and I will make you fishers of men.' At once they left their nets and followed him.
>
> (Matthew 4:18–20)

There is a calm simplicity to Matthew's telling of the story. Jesus spoke in their language. Fishing was probably all that they really understood, so a bold proclamation such as 'Come, follow me, and by my superior mentoring abilities I will make you into the best evangelists on earth' just wouldn't have worked. It strikes me that God often breaks into our worlds using our language, meeting us where we are, doing what we do. Do we do the same thing? Or do we insist that people come to where we are, and do what we're doing before we tell them about God?

Verse 18 is fantastic: 'They were casting a net into the lake, for they were fishermen.' That's deep! What else does Matthew think we are going to presume? That they were casting a net into a lake because they were underwater tennis players? But this sentence does make the important point that these guys were normal blokes. They were doing normal jobs. They hadn't been to university or got very far from home. Peter's dad, Jonah, was a fisherman too, and he had simply inherited the family business. But as anyone knows who runs even the smallest of businesses, this is seriously hard work, especially if your dad is still around! Peter was a natural leader amongst his fishing mates, and the sea would have been his life. This was all he knew. He wasn't hanging around the harbour hoping for a head-hunter from Harry Ramsden's to come along, or for the recruiting officers of the local resistance to hire him as a heavy. So why on earth would this local bloke with local responsibilities (and a wife) be vulnerable to what happened in verse 20: 'At once they left their nets and followed him'?

Many of the young people who come to work for Youth For Christ are quite literally dropping their nets because they have heard the call of Jesus. Think of what Simon Peter is leaving behind. His livelihood, his security, his wife and family, his familiar neighbourhood, his favourite fishing boat. It's not as if Jesus has given him a detailed job description, and he certainly hasn't been able to negotiate some half-days to pick up the kids from school.

Every year YFC volunteers step away from friends and family to step into uncharted waters. This can mean laying down their preferred place at university, with no guarantee that a certain course will be offered again. It can mean boyfriend–girlfriend relationships suddenly becoming 'long-distance', or their spending power being reduced substantially without parental help or part-time jobs. There must have been and there still must be something compelling about the call of this man called Jesus. Simon Peter and the others followed immediately. No questions asked. No turning back to check if it was all right with everybody else. No forwarding address. No mobile phone for safety and peace and mind. You'll see this in Lewis' twenty-first-century reality later on, but Jesus also had some further words on the subject later in Luke's Gospel:

> As they were walking along the road, a man said to him, 'I will follow you wherever you go.'

Jesus replied, 'Foxes have holes and birds of the air have nests, but the Son of Man has nowhere to lay his head.'

He said to another man, 'Follow me.'

But the man replied, 'Lord, first let me go and bury my father.'

Jesus said to him, 'Let the dead bury their own dead, but you go and proclaim the kingdom of God.'

Still another said, 'I will follow you, Lord; but first let me go back and say good-bye to my family.'

Jesus replied, 'No-one who puts his hand to the plough and looks back is fit for service in the kingdom of God.' (Luke 9:57–62)

There is a wonderful scene in the TV series *The West Wing* where a young political operative called Josh Lyman does a contemporary version of what Andrew does for his brother Simon. Josh has been working for a well-known but superficial presidential candidate, but an old friend of his father suggests he comes to hear a dark horse speaking. Josh hears this new guy speak with honesty and integrity, and straight away knows that he is 'the real thing'. He decides to change allegiance and work to get this guy elected instead. Sam, his best friend from college, is presently working as a lawyer for oil companies, but his real talents lie in speech-writing. He has previously told Josh only to come recruiting him if he has found 'the real thing'. In the middle of a board-room discussion on the safety of oil tankers, Josh only has to appear at the window of the room with a smile on his face for Sam to simply get up and walk out of the meeting. He leaves all his files on the board-room table; he leaves his colleagues behind; he leaves his boss with a gaping mouth. There is no discussion of a redundancy package. There is no apology or 'working your notice'. There is no farewell party. There is no tending to fragile relationships. Sometimes you've just got to go. Watching this scene was the first time I've seen anything similar to what it must have been like for those first disciples to simply drop everything and follow, aware of the cost to their careers and family relationships. In it there was that same sense that there is nothing and no one else worth following except 'the real thing'. And his name is Jesus. And he made it pretty clear that he wanted people's complete loyalty.

Hook, line and sinker

I wonder if our understanding of what Simon Peter understood about being a 'fisher of men' has become clouded over time. The only fishing that I observe these days is carried out by those most patient of souls who seem to just love sitting for days on end by rivers and lakes. Everything is there – tent, thermos flask and fold-away chair (with cup-holder as standard feature). When I think 'fishing', this is what I think of. Tossing out some bait, and then just sitting and waiting for hours and hours. Is this what our evangelism has become? Yes, we're expert at preparing exactly the right bait, and if someone happens to bite, then we know precisely what to do to reel them in. But this is not what Simon Peter would have had in mind. He must have been imagining high-energy, high-effort work, struggling to drag a netful of souls into the kingdom boat. He's expecting them to be wriggling and evasive, and to come in their tens and hundreds. And importantly, he's had to go looking for them, rather than the other way round. Have we sanitized our fishing? Have we turned it into an occasional, planned leisure activity or pastime, rather than a life-stretching adventure?

We also need to understand the context that these fishermen had for being a follower or disciple. In Rob Bell's book *Velvet Elvis*, he describes how only the best of the best of young Jewish scholars would make it through the various levels of Hebrew education to the point where they could ask for an interview with a Rabbi. During this interview, the Rabbi would discern if they had what it took to be one of his select followers. So can you see what a world-inverting experience it would have been for some uneducated fishermen to have a Rabbi walk straight up to them and inform them that *he* is choosing *them*! The fact that Peter was earning his living from fishing tells us straight away that he was not one of these chosen few. Yet he becomes convinced of the fact that he is chosen. Jesus will later expand on this, using the language of adoption to reinforce his point. The power of being personally called to a mission should not be underestimated. Knowing that you have a specific role is a much better motivator than responding to a generic need. How do we articulate our calls to young people?

It is worth pondering Jesus' language here for a little longer. He said, 'I will make you fishers of men.' You can bet your life that the disciples could (1) 'get inside' the image (i.e. understanding its nuances), and (2) were regularly reminded of it as they fished. It is not, however, what he says to us. Imagine if Jesus came to you in your place of work or study today and announced that he was going to involve you in his plan for the kingdom coming on earth. What would he say? What image would he use that would be relevant to you? (If you happen to be a fisherman, then this is easy!) What would he say to a journalist? Perhaps, 'I will make you a publisher of good news.' Or to an advertising executive, 'You will draw men to me.' Would it help to see your mission for God on this earth in terms of what you're passionate about, be that a football match, or a campaign against injustice, or a desire to care for children with special educational needs? Depending on your profession, those who were fish to Simon Peter could be arrested criminals, websites, or house sales to you.

Caught, not taught

In Luke's telling of the story, the call is preceded by a miraculous event:

> When he had finished speaking, he said to Simon, 'Put out into deep water, and let down the nets for a catch.'

Simon answered, 'Master, we've worked hard all night and haven't caught anything. But because you say so, I will let down the nets.'

(Luke 5:4–5)

This instruction follows Jesus' creative use of Simon's fishing boat as a makeshift pulpit. I've often wondered exactly what this must have looked like. Did he need to get in the boat because the crowd was playing the old 'back a bit further... back a little bit further... *splosh!*' gag? Isn't it interesting that the experience is recorded, but the sermon is not (unlike most of our Sunday mornings)? Did people have to strain to hear Jesus above the sound of the lapping water? Or did his voice carry such authority that, to all intents and purposes, other sound-waves and time just stood still when he spoke? It was this authority that led Simon to say in verse 5, 'because you say so, I will let down the nets', even though this statement is prefaced with the polite version of 'You must be mad. You're a preacher. You know nothing about fishing!' Jesus has also just made his authority clear through a spate of healings, and Simon knows this for sure, as one of those healed was his mother-in-law! Even this early in their relationship, a trust that is built on immense respect, and perhaps even reverence, is being displayed. The word 'Master' that Simon Peter uses is one which we find difficult to use today. In our desire for independence and self-sufficiency, we struggle to submit to any authority, never mind publicly calling someone something like 'Master'. Perhaps the idea of old-fashioned cane-waving schoolmasters leaves us with connotations of a strict disciplinarian offering no grace or depth of relationship. These things are, however, exactly what Jesus is offering to these men. They will be apprentices and he will be their Master.

I have noticed this dynamic at play with young people today. You can spend months trying to convince a young person that they are, for example, musically talented, and that they could offer those talents to God for use in his kingdom. You can explain that music can communicate in ways that mere words cannot.

You can explain that something about the mix of lyric and melody gets planted in people's memories for much longer than a purely spoken phrase. You can underline the dynamic connection between certain styles of music and their ability to transform or endorse how someone is feeling. You can do all these things, but the young person may still sit with a guitar on their lap, utterly bereft of any creativity or energy.

Now take that young person to a concert where they can see the impact of someone communicating through music, and straight away it's a different story. They feel the electricity. They see that connection that the audience is making with the artist. They look at the faces of those in the auditorium. They share the laughter or the tears. It is in those moments that you have the privilege of being grabbed by excited young people and told, 'That's what I want to do! I want to be the best guitarist/vocalist/didgeridoo-ist [delete as appropriate] I can be!' Months of attempting to sell a concept have been trumped by a few moments of seeing it in action.

I suspect this is how the disciples were feeling. I would want to follow someone who was presently the life and soul of the Galilean party. I would want to learn a few tricks from someone who was healing diseases in a way I could never have thought possible. I would want to be an apprentice to this Master.

So how do we best communicate kingdom living to our young people? In light of these thoughts, the answer seems pretty obvious: by modelling kingdom living to them. Even if they don't know it, young people are desperate to see us fleshing out the values of the kingdom. They are desperate for role models, and so when the church doesn't provide any, they're left with what they see on MTV, or read in the pages of celebrity magazines. You could call what has been going on a dereliction of duty on the part of the church. Tell you what, then – we'll pay someone (let's call him a youth worker) to do that for us. That'll be handier and much less messy, actually.

There is a common misconception that to be an effective role model for young people these days, you have to be young and cool yourself. Not so. Young people sniff out pretence in an instant. What they want to know is if this person is in it for the long haul with me. Jesus made it clear that he was going to journey *with* the disciples.

Years ago I met an amazing man called Gerald, who every week at a youth club would put the chairs out, sell drinks all night and afterwards tidy things away. He would chat with any of the young people who came over to him, even if he had to strain to hear over the dance music that was pumping from the stereo. He modelled service and hospitality to those young people in a way that I never could. He was a dependable constant in their lives, and they would end up letting him in on their successes and failures, whether they were talking about exams, relationships or sport. Gerald was seventy-four years old. It wasn't his cool haircut or nose-ring that made him relevant. It was his heart.

Washing the car

I can't leave the subject of discipleship without telling you about what, for me, has been the most significant shift in my understanding of it in recent years. Peter has adventured with Jesus and therefore knows him better. Only once we have worked with him, travelled with him and seen his power, do we know who he truly is. Bart Campolo put this in stark context for me when he told a story similar to mine that follows.

Do you remember, as young boy, being asked by your dad to help wash the car? Or (to be horrendously gender-stereotypical) do you remember your mum asking you to help in the kitchen, making buns or scones? I remember my excitement at moments like that. Not only was the thought of getting utterly covered in soapy suds quite fantastic, but there was a glowing pride that my dad needed my help to wash the car. Dad needs me! It felt good. It was often the highlight of my Saturday afternoon.

Only with the benefit of hindsight have I come to realize that I almost certainly made the whole process last much longer, and my sections of the car probably didn't get washed as well as the parts my dad had been working on. So in light of this, why did my dad ask for my help? I've come to the undeniable conclusion that my dad asked for my help because he wanted me to be where he was. He wanted me to be doing what he was doing. He wanted to simply get to know me better in the midst of a shared task.

Does that not shine a halogen-powered light into our understanding of our manic activity? We flit around believing that God needs our help to save the world, when our Father is very simply asking us to be getting up to what he's up to. Because all over this world God is, by his Spirit, healing the sick, releasing the oppressed and bringing good news to the poor, and he simply asks us to join him. He doesn't need our help, but he asks us to wash the car with him. He wants us to be with him. We have reduced knowing God to an academic, silent exercise. How do you really get to know people? The strongest relationships are formed in the fire of a shared activity or task, be that at work, or at play. Our knowing of him grows in the doing. If we're not engaging with him in serving the poor and the needy, then there are aspects of his character we will simply never get to know.

In this respect today's young people are miles ahead of previous generations. They are experiencing the reality of working with God in their communities and so building genuine working relationships with him. Their knowing is growing in their doing. They have left behind the old modernist notion that first we learn something, then we go out and do it. Young people are getting caught up in the adventure of seeing a world changed, and in the process they are getting to know its creator. So, in a beautiful inversion of my story, let's roll up our sleeves and grab a sponge.

Drowning in the shallows

I don't think it is a coincidence that Jesus tells Simon Peter to put out into 'deep water'. Right at the start of his journey with the disciples, Jesus is underlining that this is not going to be a journey without cost or effort. There is inevitable danger associated with deep water. The flags and lifeguard stations around the coasts of the UK pay testimony to that. If you are tossed from a boat in deep water, then you had better be able to swim, or at least float (assuming that you have something to float with!).

Even if we can't swim, most of us love water. Many people dream of retiring to a house by the sea, so they can stare out across its beauty and walk by the shore. But I fear that's as far as many of us get. It's very easy to experience something of the sea without actually experiencing the sea. It's called paddling. Paddling takes a lot less effort than actually getting into the sea to swim. You don't have to bother with taking your clothes off. You don't have to put sun cream on. You don't have to swallow any salty water, and your eyes certainly won't sting! Yes, you'll feel the wonderful coolness of the water moulding itself around your toes, and the tickle of the last rites of a breaker, but are you missing out?

It's very easy to 'just do enough' in our service to the church and the young people who are part of it. We can pay our money and sing the songs, but could Jesus be calling us out into the deep water, where we might actually have to swim? It's very easy to find a comfort zone in any institution. We do enough to get by but never let ourselves be stretched. Could we do that talk for the youth group, or be a leader for their weekend away? Sure, it may leave us gasping for air, but I've discovered something really important recently. It's only when I swim that I truly feel alive. I'm using all of my muscles, stretching my lung capacity and knowing the powerful sensation of my limbs and trunk cutting through the water. The challenges that being around young people brings will not make us more comfortable but could surely make us feel more alive. Or will we be left drowning in the shallows?

This is a prayer I wrote recently, when I was feeling that I had been paddling around for too long at the edge:

So lead me to your depths
Immerse me gently there
For freedom comes from dying
Then coming up for air.

This deep water resonates with what we know about baptism and its symbolism. Jesus has just experienced it first-hand. In his letter to the Philippians, Paul puts it like this:

I want to know Christ and the power of his resurrection and the fellowship of sharing in his sufferings, becoming like him in his death, and so, some-how, to attain to the resurrection from the dead.   (Philippians 3:10–11)

To truly follow Christ out into the deep water, as Simon Peter will do, will lead us to the place of sharing in his sufferings. These sufferings will be a dying to ourselves, with the promise of resurrection. The truth that no one is promising us an easy life in the deep water is being underlined. The problem is that we employ 'suffering-avoidance' procedures to stay out of the deep water, so we don't experience the true depth of being disciples. We avoid awkward people and awkward places. We steer away from engaging with the poor, beyond the ease of writing cheques. Being submerged is not a lot of fun, but that first gasp of breath when you come crashing back through the surface of the water is a truly wonderful moment. Death gives way to life.

Simon Peter's roller-coaster life is teaching us that we will have moments of pain and struggle if we truly choose to journey with Jesus, rather than just watch him from a safe distance on the shoreline. The reassuring thing is that, as Paul reminds us again in Colossians, this cross-channel swim is fuelled by a higher power:

> We proclaim him, admonishing and teaching everyone with all wisdom, so that we may present everyone perfect in Christ: to this end I labour, struggling with all his energy, which so powerfully works in me.
>
> (Colossians 1:28–29)

The words 'struggling with all his energy' stick out of those verses for me. How often does my breathing become laboured, and how often do my muscles go floppy because I have been struggling with all *my* energy rather than with his. That's why I run back to the shallows.

Face on the floor

You probably know the rest of the story. The catch that ensued broke the Galilee all-comers record, and very nearly broke their nets. They scraped through with the aid of a nearby boat, but even then the boats started to sink! This makes it all the more amazing that the conscientious, pragmatic fisherman we call Simon Peter is not at this point working on a plan to get this miracle catch to shore. He's not barking instructions as he normally would in a crisis scenario. He's not throwing his muscular frame into awe-inspiring action. Where is he? He's on his face:

> When Simon Peter saw this, he fell at Jesus' knees and said, 'Go away from me, Lord; I am a sinful man!' For he and all his companions were astonished at the catch of fish they had taken.   (Luke 5:8–9)

What Simon Peter had just experienced changed his life. It made all the difference. Yes, he was thinking, all the healings were impressive (but you can never over-estimate the power of positive thinking), and yes, the fever left his mother-in-law (even though he wasn't necessarily over the moon about that one!). But this simply took everything to a whole new level. He had been working his socks off (though I doubt he wore them in the boat) all night, and not one fish had so much as teased him with its presence. There was no natural explanation for what he had just seen. It was quite literally supernatural. It left Peter in no doubt that he was in the presence of the divine. He was breathing in the same air as the Holy One of God. Being in the holy presence of God immediately makes us aware of our own sinfulness. He knew he was in the presence of royalty, so he dropped to his knees. And this was not mere earthly royalty, but the King of all kings.

But to claim that all this intellectual processing was going on is to exaggerate the situation. Simon Peter simply hit the deck because he could do nothing else. It was a natural, beautiful reflex. How wonderful that this moment was also the moment of his calling, as Jesus said, 'Don't be afraid; from now on you will catch men.' The bottom line is that the most important catch that day was Simon Peter himself.

Following on from men like Isaiah, who heard the call in that place of holiness, today's disciples also hear that same voice when they take the time to stop and listen. Lewis in the next chapter is one such guy.

4 Sat-nav

Lewis

Sitting there trembling in his seat, with the whole room buzzing around him, Lewis wondered why the entire place suddenly felt so weird. He was used to evangelistic meetings. His Christian upbringing had made this sort of stuff a regular part of his life. Why was tonight any different? Why did he feel like there was a spotlight directly on him? The evangelist's words pounded deep into his soul in a way that no preacher's words had ever done before. Lewis was cemented to his seat, digesting and agreeing with every word, utterly oblivious to everything and everyone else around him.

As he stared forward into the bright lights, he felt something stirring in his spirit. This preacher didn't seem to follow the normal pattern – there weren't any warm-up jokes or funny stories to keep things light.

He got straight to the meat of what he wanted to say, and Lewis was convicted right from the start. 'God has done everything for me, and I have done nothing for him!' He couldn't get away from that one thought. Then, before he had time to think further, an audible voice came out of nowhere: 'Lewis, I want you to be an evangelist working with young people.' He knew that it was God speaking to him because he would never, in a million years, have come up with such a crazy idea. As far as he was concerned, he was going to finish college, then train to be a friendly teacher. Being an evangelist was not on his agenda. It didn't make any sense. There was nothing special about him. He was the sort of guy who was happy to follow the latest trends, but he would never set them. He was your solid organizer – the completer/finisher of the team. He was also in no rush to put his skinny physique on show on a platform anytime soon!

At his church the next day Lewis' attention was grasped again by the sermon, and he felt what he could only describe as pins and needles, up and down his body. The preacher was talking about running the race for God and passing on the baton to the next generation. Deep down Lewis knew that God was speaking to him again, confirming his new direction, but he was scared. The idea had literally come from nowhere, and Lewis was not convinced that he was the man for the job. He spent the next week or so blocking out the words and feelings, trying to rationalize his thoughts and rekindle a desire for teaching.

It didn't work. Before he had time to forget, a bundle of mail fell through his letter-box. The letter that he picked up first detailed an opportunity in youth work and evangelism. 'How did they get my address?' he thought. He had no memory of registering with them, and immediately wondered if this was the next link in the chain. He emailed the organization and a note came back:

> If this is where you are called to be, then great, but don't be afraid to explore other options. Let the gift of evangelism be fanned into flame at college with your friends, and then see what happens.

Lewis was disappointed that they hadn't encouraged him to join them and, in all honesty, he felt that their reply was a polite way of saying no.

But now that he had tasted the future, he was hungry to explore different opportunities. The desire to see what was out there was greater than his fear of the unknown. As he scanned the internet, he remembered an event earlier in the year where he was handed a leaflet about evangelistic opportunities with Youth For Christ. He had become a Christian at the same event a year before, and logged in his mind was a conversation with a YFC leader called Dave. He had been greatly influential in Lewis finding Jesus and had given him the leaflet. Lewis dug out the tatty old form from a drawer, and thereby he found the YFC website.

'Gap year opportunities in youth work and evangelism' headlined the homepage. As he scrolled down, the e.t.a. course (evangelism, training, action) immediately grabbed Lewis' attention and the pins and needles reappeared. He filled out the form online, got the information pack through the post within two days, and read every detail straight away. He knew it was what he was meant to be doing. Lewis' Mum was a bit unsure about his decision. 'I really thought you wanted to be a teacher,' she commented. For the first time, Lewis allowed his thoughts to be spoken aloud: 'I did. But I really believe that God is calling me into youth work and evangelism.' By speaking it out, he could feel himself taking ownership of God's plan for his life. His church was very supportive of his decision to apply to YFC, and their willingness to financially stand with him was another signal to Lewis that he was doing the right thing.

At his interview some of the old fear returned, and even though he knew he was being obedient to God's voice, he really wasn't sure how effective he would be in what was expected of him.

He was also worried that he had answered the questions a little bit too honestly. The interviewer had asked him, 'So what made you apply to join YFC?'

'Well, I'm not quite sure. I just felt that I should,' he replied.

'So why do you want to do youth work and evangelism?' the interviewer shot back.

'I'm not sure I do,' Lewis answered.

The next question carried a hint of frustration: 'So why are you here?'

He scrambled his thoughts together and replied in the only way he could: 'Because I believe that God wants me to be here. He wants me to tell my peers about Jesus before it is too late.'

Even though he was nervous, the interviewers clearly saw Lewis' heart and passion for lost young people, and they affirmed God's calling on his life. Yes, he had been honest but it had paid off. The doors opened and Lewis was accepted onto the gap year.

As he completed his final year of college, waiting to get stuck in on the youth-work training programme, his life grew more difficult. He hadn't been expecting challenges. He had made his decision. He had heard from God and so it was all sorted, wasn't it? Yet there was a niggling feeling in his mind. He couldn't shake the subconscious desire to 'live it up a bit' before settling into this new life for God. Even though Lewis' conscience kept telling him that God wanted him to be 'set apart' from the old crowd, it was easier said than done. He partied pretty hard with his friends, drinking regularly and convincing himself that it was OK for now. He found himself involved in a questionable relationship with a girl who wasn't a Christian and he struggled to find a way out.

It wasn't until Soul Survivor's summer conference that Lewis finally sorted his life out for good. At the end of one of the main meetings he went forward for prayer. After standing alone for a while, he felt his palms go sweaty and his mind play tricks on him: 'Are you sure you need prayer?' said a voice in his head. 'You'll get through this without it. It won't make much of a difference.'

Lewis wondered if he should return to his friends at the back, but just as he opened his eyes to locate them, a hand came to rest firmly on his shoulder. There was no time to question now. He knew he was in the right place because the words that were being spoken over him and into his life resonated in his heart and mind: 'God says that because of what you are about to do for him, something in your life needs to change. You need to break away from an unhelpful situation.'

These words were enough for Lewis. After the meeting had ended, he headed back to his tent. Locating his mobile phone under his pillow, he quickly rang his girlfriend. He ended the relationship as kindly as he could, knowing inside that it was the best thing for both of them. Then he spent the rest of the week drawing near to God once more.

That autumn he began his year all fired up. Placed in Worthing on the south coast, he got stuck into working with kids and sharing his faith. It was a life-changing experience. He began the gap year as a relatively quiet individual who lacked confidence in his ability, but bit by bit, through lots of little challenges, he stepped out of his comfort zones, trusting that God was in control. Through schools work, sharing one-to-one and preaching, Lewis grew in his faith and in his belief in himself. He'd had the privilege of seeing many young people meet Jesus. By the end of the year he was prepared to try anything. He was convinced of his calling to youth work and evangelism, and he was confident in his gifts. As the year was drawing to an end, he made plans to stay in Worthing for another year.

Unbeknown to him, God had other plans, and was about to steer him in another direction. Lewis joined the rest of his team for an end-of-year mission in the Midlands and worked incredibly well with another team member running a skate-park. On the last night, one of the leaders approached Lewis and said, 'Maybe you're not meant to continue working down south. Perhaps you're supposed to be working on the Missions team. I think you need to test it and make sure.'

Lewis was frozen to the spot. He suddenly felt confused, and he couldn't shake off the words that had been spoken. He felt that if staying down south was definitely right, then he would have been able to say so, and known why, but instead he was suddenly consumed with a list of reasons why it might be wrong to return. He began to wonder whether staying in the same location for a second year would be too comfortable, and if God wanted to push him even further out of his comfort zone.

Over the next few days Lewis sought counsel and prayed with various people, also getting more information about the Missions team. It was definitely going to be challenging: three big missions in three different cities in one year, with a team of four preparing each location before the full team arrived. They would make contacts with local churches, raise expectation levels and ensure that follow-up was organized for those who came to faith. The strange thing was that Dave, the YFC guy whom he had met years earlier, was now overseeing the Missions team.

Decision-making wasn't so straightforward this time. The team in Worthing were gutted that Lewis was considering not returning. His family were not convinced by this sudden change in direction, and his Mum became quite upset. Lewis began to realize that sometimes when God guides you, not everyone is on board with his plans. Even the people closest to you can be left sitting in the departure lounge. He was also learning that sometimes it's right to do some thinking around decisions, rather than simply going with your gut. Despite the problems he was encountering, Lewis felt that the Missions team was looking like the right way ahead. He really desired some kind of further confirmation.

It didn't take long to get it. At another church service, he was listening to a speaker and yet again, he had that 'all eyes are on me' feeling. The speaker was talking about getting out of the boat – leaving your comfort zones and fixing your eyes on Jesus. She went on to say: 'Some of you are trying to make choices tonight about your future – maybe you are not stepping out because you are being held back by something or you are scared.' At the end of the talk, Lewis stood to acknowledge that that was where he was at. As he was prayed for, the guy praying with him said, 'The Lord tells you to go.' He couldn't ask for any more. That night he thanked God from the bottom of his heart and, despite upsetting the church in Worthing, he joined the Missions team.

Since Lewis' year spent serving on the Missions team, God's guidance hasn't always been so clear and direct, but Lewis still knows for sure that God has a plan for his life. He has realized that sometimes God uses the big audible voice to get our attention, but once he has you in his boat, he may change the way in which he directs you. When you are on the right general course, it only takes a gentle nudge of the rudder to send you in the right direction.

When the Missions team was drawing to an end, a series of circumstances led Lewis to begin training for a degree in youth ministry. The 'gentle nudges' came through being handed a folder of possible youth-work courses, having a conversation with a friend who had been on one of the courses, and praying with a mentor. These things, and the desire to keep serving young people, were enough to push him towards the degree. If he had waited for another audible voice, it may not have come, and an opportunity could have been wasted.

Lewis learnt not to assume, just because the sky is blue and the wind is up, that it's the right time to set sail. He started to see that God's timing and perspective on his life were often not the same as his.

He's now learning, watching and waiting for the breeze.

5 Checking Your Mirror

Jemima

Have you ever found yourself sitting somewhere quietly, observing everything else going on around you? You look at the people, watching what they are doing, letting yourself slowly drift into the background. The more you watch them, the more talented, capable and popular they appear to be. You, however, convince yourself that you have absolutely nothing to offer, that you are lacking that 'X factor', and that no one would bother to give you a second look.

This was a common occurrence for Jemima. She felt like she spent most of her days observing the talented hopefuls who would soar through the first round, making it to the 'X factor' boot-camp. She, however, was the girl standing in front of Simon Cowell with no confidence, desperate to present herself in such a way as to be recognized and believed in. Every day in school felt like a compressed version of the show – she was there performing, keen to make the grade, but never quite fitting the mould that was required.

This lack of self-esteem was something that Jemima had battled with for as long as she could remember, and no matter how hard she tried, she could not shift gear in her mind from the constant belief that all the people at school were more worthy of attention than she was. Deep down something told her that there was no point in her having a go at anything, because there would always be someone else who could do it better. There wasn't anything in her life that she excelled in. She could run, but not very fast; she could play 'Chopsticks', but she would never master Mozart; and her drawings looked no better than the figures on toilet doors. Jemima lived in a land called mediocrity and she knew that however hard she tried to cross the border, there would always be an imposing soldier staring at her passport, then shaking his head.

Being in a small school within a confined group of friends made it very difficult for Jemima to see herself from a broader perspective. She was a victim of a teenage environment that gave everyone a label, even if they didn't want one. Her peers all wore the same uniform, but little details revealed the clique they belonged to: the thick red lipstick, the hair gel, socks rolled neatly down, skirts shifted up over the knee, small tightly knotted ties with only the small end on display, sums scribbled onto the backs of hands, black nails and skull rings – these were the subtle flags that marked out the different territories within each year group. But Jemima's friends wore nothing unusual. Their uniform looked normal – their skirts reached their knees, their ties were knotted properly and their socks were wrinkle free. Jemima felt that the group that she had fallen into restricted her from being herself – or even discovering who she could be.

Rarely did anyone break out of their position in the pecking order. Even if someone did, you didn't take much notice because they would soon be back in their old mould. One of the girls in her group had dated a guy in the football team, shortening her skirt to fit in with the other girlfriends. It didn't last long. He was ribbed for going out with her, she couldn't keep up with the lives they lived, and she soon ended up back where she 'belonged'. Jemima's only hope was that getting away from this school would help her find the real Jemima.

In some ways she was right. Moving to sixth form college for her 'A' levels did change things a bit. When she walked into her tutor group halfway through her first week, she literally felt like she was starting again with a clean slate. There were no beady, judging eyes, giving her the once-over, but rather a relaxed bunch of people smiling and chatting together.

The difference wasn't purely external. She may have had her own set of issues but she now also had God in her life to help her through them. She hadn't realized he was there at first, and, to be honest, she hadn't realized she had any problems either, but now she was beginning to see her life more clearly. She had been invited to a church youth group, and meeting some people who were Christians showed her the truth of who she really was.

In the past the Bible had seemed irrelevant to her personal life, but now she was beginning to take hold of verses and believe them. Psalm 139:14 was one that she began to speak over herself whenever her confidence was rocked: 'I praise you because I am fearfully and wonderfully made; your works are wonderful, I know that full well.'

As Jemima began to grasp how God really felt about her, she changed more and more. She knew that knowing him meant that she had so much more than the people around her, and it was something that they desperately needed. Jemima felt like shackles had been taken off and she became much happier with herself.

As she slowly changed internally, she began to behave differently towards those around her. Feeling more secure in her own identity, she could recognize and point out the talents and abilities in others. And the strange thing was that she was enjoying doing this. She was also increasingly aware of people who were struggling, and frequently she found herself listening to their problems. When one girl took an overdose and came to Jemima for counsel and help, she found herself able to listen and ready to care. She started to accept that people liked her. They not only liked her, they trusted her, and she knew that trust was not easy to come by. Girls would by-pass conversations with their closest pals to seek out her concern and advice. They clearly saw something steadfast and reliable in Jemima's life, and slowly, she began to see those things in herself too.

Becoming the kind of person who opened up and shared her life with those around her encouraged others to do the same. She was honest about struggling with her weight and self-confidence and was very surprised to find out that the majority of her friends had similar feelings about themselves. The more she talked, listened, cared and counselled, the more Jemima accepted that her observations of life at school had been viewed through a distorted lens. Seeing the effect of using her 'natural gifts' enabled her to realize that people weren't always what she thought they were. In actual fact, everyone struggled with something. Jemima noticed that it didn't matter how far up the 'talented' ladder you climbed, there was always someone above you. The most popular girl at school may have been beautiful and intelligent, with lots of boys after her, but that seemed to make her even more obsessed about her looks. The fantastic musician may have played amazing solos from the stage, but he vomited in the toilets beforehand. The lights were slowly coming on in Jemima's head and despite still struggling with her own self-image, she realized that she wasn't alone.

After her first few months at college, Jemima knew that despite her insecurities, she wanted to share God with other people. She was made in the image of God, but so were all these other young people, but they just didn't know it yet. Reading 1 Corinthians 12 had revealed to her that she was an important part of God's plan – he had created her for a purpose and had given her gifts to enable her to encourage others. Now she wanted to go back to school and share these truths with the lost cliques gathering in the corridors and halls.

Amazingly, the desire in her heart was fulfilled. Her former head of year invited her back in to take a few Christmas assemblies. Apparently he was a Christian, and he knew someone at her church who raved about the changes in Jemima's life, so he wanted her to share these with the rest of the school. This was a major opportunity but also terrifying. To go back into the environment that she had just left and talk about her faith openly with people who still recognized her face, who had looked down on her, and who had been far more popular than her, was frightening. The more she thought about it, the more her insecurities rose to the surface, but she couldn't let the opportunity pass by.

As Jemima took to the stage she looked down at the cliques of pupils. The different continents spread across the school hall stared back at her. At first she panicked, but a revelation quickly came that brought her peace: No longer was she in the midst of them, trying to work out which race, creed or colour she belonged to. Now she was up here, on top of the world, free from the identity crisis and sure of who she was. It gave her comfort – firstly to know that she wasn't the only one who had been a victim of their environment, but secondly to know that she belonged to God and that she had the unusual privilege of helping them to find him too.

Despite the giggling in the front row and the empty faces looking up at her, Jemima confidently challenged the school about the real meaning of Christmas. She talked about how quickly the roast turkey disappears and how presents are hastily opened and then forgotten. 'Jesus, on the other hand, will never leave you. He wants a relationship with you for ever,' she announced clearly into the microphone.

A teacher who had known Jemima for six years was blown away by the change in her, and told her to make sure that she continued to nurture the skills she was developing. Jemima really sensed God saying, 'You can do this. Yes, it's frightening stuff and stepping out is hard, but you will know you are doing a good job because I'm going to keep telling you that.'

A few months passed, and her former head of year rang again. 'We were very impressed with your Christmas assemblies last year and would love to have you back to do some other things.' Later that month she found herself taking an assembly for Years 10 and 11 (aged 14 to 16) about self-esteem. Again she stood in front of the pupils, with a further increase in confidence, and began to tell her own story. All eyes were on her, especially those of the girls, as she wore her heart on her sleeve, explaining how she used to see herself as worthless and mediocre at everything. She talked about comparing herself with others and thinking that she had nothing to give. 'God changed everything for me,' she shared. 'He doesn't think we are worthless – in fact, we are all special to him. If he can increase my self-esteem, he can increase yours.'

God had called Jemima to step out, and even though it was difficult, he had gradually prepared her for it. She didn't see any dramatic changes in people's lives following the assembly, but the constant eye contact, the knowing looks and the smiles were enough to convince her that people had connected with what she had said. She understood that she would never know the impact of that assembly, but she had reached a place where she knew that she had to talk about her faith, trusting that she was faithfully serving God.

She was learning to be grateful for her God-given gifts. Whereas previously, if anyone had complimented her, she would have been quick to disregard it, Jemima was now able to say thank you.

It was around this time that Jemima heard about Youth For Christ and their gap-year teams. It took a real step of faith for her to apply to join e.t.a. (evangelism, training, action), as she feared that she wasn't 'good enough', but she was accepted onto the programme. Over the next year Jemima had the opportunity to use her gifts further and to see the effects of serving as part of a team. When her team-mate Ally had a problem with one of the lads on the team, Jemima sat down with the two of them and helped them to work it out. When she knew that another e.t.a. gap-year student was struggling, she would text an encouraging Bible verse to them. Jemima thrived in her new environment. She loved working with Year 7 students (aged 11 to 12) in lunch-time clubs, because she could recognize the potential in each one, behind their masks. She was able to run a Rock Solid Club (YFC's outreach resource for 11–14s) with the same young people and train them up to be young leaders themselves. She invested in them over coffee – listening to their struggles, offering advice and helping them to know God better.

At times during the gap year she thought, 'What's the point of meeting with them?' They seemed to change so slowly, and she wasn't sure that they really wanted to be there. She was learning that young people often don't give you any feedback or encouragement while you're working with them. She realized that her questions were probably still triggered by her own insecurities and she just needed to stay committed to what God had called her to do, accepting affirmation from him.

One by one the young people recognized the dependable listening gifts in Jemima and began to open up about their hopes and fears in the space created by her non-judgmental welcome. Susan was a girl who suffered with insecurity in the midst of her stick-thin friends. As she downloaded to Jemima, even the sense that someone else understood was already making her feel better. Jemima encouraged Susan to spend time telling herself that she was beautiful. Instead of being scared or ashamed to look in the mirror, she should look at herself in a new light, trying to see what God sees: a woman made in his image. Jemima suggested that Susan should read some specific scriptures like Psalm 139, to find out who she was, and meditate on them often, allowing God's truth to sink in.

These concepts caused Susan to develop other ways of helping herself. She made a collage of pictures, each one depicting herself at a different point in her life. Through this she learned to be pleased with how she appeared and how God saw her. Jemima was blown away as she witnessed the girl's self-image dramatically improve. She couldn't believe that little-old-her had played a part in Susan's transformation and that God had chosen to use her in this girl's life.

As Jemima sits down for coffee with the new Susan, she smiles. Jemima knows that, despite her insecurities rearing their ugly heads at times, God still has a plan for her life. She is sure that he will continue to use her, enabling her to listen with his ears.

She looks up from her mug and says, 'I'm glad you could make it today. How are things going with you?'

Jemima knows it's a simple question, and she realizes that society may not put her gifts on a pedestal, but equally she knows that using them can unleash effects that last a lifetime.

6 Breakdown

Rebecca

Things at home seemed to be floating along fine. Granted, they weren't the most conventional family – Dad had left a few years before and things had been painful for a long time, but Mum had somehow pulled things together. Life had gone on and the family had eventually found a relatively comfortable rhythm. Rebecca seemed to be coping well with the stress of up-coming GCSEs and her younger brother was happy at school.

A change occurred literally overnight. Rebecca first noticed little comments and mannerisms, but she tried to shrug them off. Anyway, she had exams to focus on right now; she couldn't let her mother's behaviour bother her. But no matter how hard she tried, she was unable to ignore the change in her mother's face. She told herself to keep her head down and study, because that way she didn't have to look up into her eyes, but their close relationship made it impossible not to. Rebecca could no longer see her relaxed smile, which extended to the tiny lines around her eyes. In its place was a deep, distressed furrow across her brow that never shifted. Instead of looking happy and contented, Mum looked confused and, although it was hard to believe, mildly aggressive.

Rebecca sat at her desk, pulling her blonde hair out of her face, trying to focus on the equations staring back at her. She was desperately trying to make sense of them, but they were blurring together into a stew of numbers and letters. Her studies hadn't been helped by the sleepless nights caused by relentless worry about her mother. Even now she could hear the faint tapping that she wanted to believe was coming from next door. A few days ago, she had gathered up the courage to find out what it was, and it shook her to the core to witness her mother hitting her hands insanely against the walls.

Rebecca couldn't make sense of the behaviour, so she tried to ignore what was happening. She shielded her brother from it as much as possible, and dug herself deep into her own life. She went to church and believed in God, but kept Sundays separate from the rest of her life. She deliberately chose not to work out where God was in all that was going on at home. To anyone who met Rebecca briefly, they would never guess that this pretty, popular and sporty girl carried around the weight that she did. Her independence meant she didn't really want anyone else's help. As far as she was concerned, the three of them would get through this one together.

But eventually things got out of control. Mum didn't actually lash out at them, but a series of weird episodes, where she would either stare into space or launch into manic activity, made her extremely difficult to live with. Just before Rebecca's first GCSE exam, the doctor diagnosed epilepsy and admitted her mother to hospital for treatment. Just sixteen years old, Rebecca found herself at home without either parent, having to present a motherly front to her younger brother. With her father living far away and her grandmother on holiday, she had no other choice but to attempt to cope with what was happening. She spent the next few weeks cooking whatever she could, shopping, tidying the house, visiting Mum and grabbing time to revise. She had never experienced stress until now: the disrupted sleep, the mind full of things that she had to do, and a sudden load of emotions that she struggled to channel. Lying in bed with a banging head and a desire to sleep for eternity, Rebecca dreamt of the day when all this would be over and everything would be OK again.

Unfortunately that wasn't to be. Life was never going to be exactly how Rebecca remembered it. After some weeks, even though she was still suffering from mood swings, Mum was permitted to return home. Rebecca thought that this was exactly what she wanted and that it would resolve everything, but things were different now. Mum had developed a dependency on her daughter.

Through these difficult months Rebecca never questioned the existence of God. Sunday school teaching from a young age had drilled into her that God was with her through the good times and the bad times, and Rebecca accepted that.

After much soul-searching about leaving her mother behind, Rebecca accepted a place at university to study physiotherapy. She tried not to focus on her mother's health and prevented herself from pondering why God had chosen not to heal her. Even though she wanted to bury her head in the sand, imagining that Mum was better, her love for her family kept her in constant contact. Each day she would check in with home to see how Mum was, listening to reports of her seizures and constant struggles. Sometimes she would talk vaguely to her friends about the situation, but in the main she got on with things, convincing herself that it would come to an end soon and all would be well.

As time passed, things became strained. The old philosophy of 'head down, keep going' was taking its toll, and nothing was getting resolved. In fact, things were worse. As Rebecca matured, her awareness grew. Mum trusted her more and more with the state of her health, and would increasingly spend ear-aching lengths of time on the phone pouring her heart out to her daughter. As she listened to the pain and anxiety in her mother's voice, Rebecca began to realize that her mother had no control over herself. Her condition and the medication were causing her to have weird, dangerous thoughts and increasing episodes of auditory and visual hallucinations. She would find herself wandering round to people's houses with a desire to cause them harm. Rebecca's increased knowledge and understanding of her mother's illness caused an even greater dependency – her mother relied on her constant support. And even if Rebecca wanted to, she couldn't avoid learning the danger signs. She knew when Mum was struggling, and when she was holding things back from her.

Rebecca was holed up in halls, feeling deeply lonely. Gone was the support of Christian friends and mentors that she had never really taken advantage of, but had become accustomed to. In their place was a challenging course and a building full of people she did not know, and who

didn't know God. Rebecca had thought things were going to get easier –
a new course, new friends, and something to work towards, but the
opposite was happening.

Pressures, pain and loneliness were covering her like a black cloud,
and in this place, she began to wonder where God really was. She could-
n't see him at work anywhere or in anything. Why wasn't he intervening
in her life and in her mother's life? To cope with the loneliness, she
shifted the focus from herself to her mother's state of health. In the past
she had chosen not to face up to her mother's illness, but now she realized that the pain and heartache that they had walked through together
had made them closer than ever.

At this point Rebecca was informed that her mother's condition had
worsened. The more she heard about the illness, the more her doubt in
God's existence grew. How could these things possibly happen to someone who loved God and wanted to follow him? She began to become very
worried about what might happen next. She worried about her mother's
safety – she wondered if she was having suicidal thoughts. She also
knew that if her mother ended up hurting someone else, the guilt that
would be unleashed could be crippling. The thoughts in her mother's
head were things that Rebecca couldn't control. Anything could happen.

She hadn't noticed it before, but now it was dawning on her that her
faith in God had been her mother's faith and her friends' faith. She had
accepted it because that was all she knew. She had never made the journey of discovering faith for herself. Now here she was, questioning
everything she had been told. Into the sky she yelled, 'God, are you really
in control?' She began to doubt every year of her faith, thinking, 'If God
isn't here now, has he ever been here? Have the things that I've

witnessed really been the work of God?' In her empty, quiet room, where sleepless nights had become the norm, Rebecca let her mind wander down a path that was unfamiliar and terrifying.

During the early hours of a cold winter night, she tried to recall moments in her life when God had shown her that he was real. She failed. She had never known a flash of light from the sky triggering her belief in Jesus. Had she accepted it all too quickly? Maybe it had just been something to fill a hole. Couldn't she just try to live a good life? Little doubts formed into a big train of doubt that was gaining speed by the second. The tunnel was long and dark.

Occasionally Rebecca tried to pray for her mother, but she didn't feel any response from God. She began to lose hope, but something inside prevented her from giving up completely. Even though she was consumed with questions, she still had old Christian friends whose lives she could not ignore. Their lives were producing strong evidence that kept making her think, 'There has got to be something more to life, but I'm not sure what it is.' She was drawn to their happiness, fulfilment and hopefulness. Their belief had made a real, radical difference to their lives. In Rebecca's mind the jury was still out, but in the midst of her questioning she knew that one way or another she would have to reach a verdict.

Rebecca decided in her heart that she couldn't give up on faith. After all, her mother hadn't. Even in her darkest moments, Mum had held onto her belief in God and had continued to go to church. If she could persevere through such pain, then surely Rebecca should keep trying to find out why. Anyway, if Jesus was real, she didn't want to risk disappointing him any more. She wondered if disowning him would mean that he would disown her too. More than anything, she wanted this 'God thing' to shift from simply being in her head to being a relationship. She started to read lots of Christian books. *The Case for Christ* by Lee Strobel was a massive help, enabling her to start from scratch, piecing the truth together for herself. She watched the Wattoto African Children's Choir sing their little hearts out at a Christian conference, and was overcome by the joy and hope flowing from them. As she sat there listening to powerful voices erupting from tiny swaying bodies, God dramatically touched her heart and emotion rose to the surface. So many feelings that she had suppressed for so long were being unleashed in an overwhelming way. Rebecca had no control over the emotion, and for the first time she had no desire to keep it all bottled up inside. She freely allowed her body to shake as the hot, salty tears streamed down her face. She wasn't quite sure why she was crying but when her puffy cheeks began to dry up hours later, she felt strangely relieved. As she reflected on what had happened, she realized that the hope of these African children had given her a sense of hope too.

There were just too many lights in Rebecca's darkness. She found the faith of those little children and her friends impossible to ignore. Her mother's consistent commitment to God, in the face of such great adversity, also had a huge impact on her. As she coupled this with the truths she found in the Bible and various other books, Rebecca found Christ for herself. No, she didn't have all the answers, but she suspected that nobody did. The journey so far had taught her that she had to hold onto the hope of forever. She would rather live with hope in Jesus, than with no hope at all.

7 Changing Lanes

Shaun

No words are being exchanged. Both sets of eyes are glued to the screen, all available fingers and thumbs dancing viciously over the control pads. 'One more minute left. I'm losing again,' thinks Shaun. 'They think it's all over, and... it is now.' Another grubby young lad is rejoicing. 'This flippin' Playstation – they always beat me!' Shaun keeps the thought to himself. For the hundredth time that afternoon 'Continue?' flashes up on the screen and he reluctantly passes his control pad onto the next player. He turns to watch the other lads tumbling around the room, reproducing the kicks and moves they've seen on screen.

With one eye on the lads and the other on the game, Shaun finds himself falling into a relaxed daze. He sees so much of himself in these lads. He thinks back to his old life in Liverpool, growing up with the 'wrong crowd' in Bootle.

It all started as he approached the gates of his new school, aged eleven. As he observed the crowd of pupils swarming in around him, he began to digest his new environment. On noting the graffiti-filled walls, the chipped paint-work, the litter strewn everywhere and the hard faces eyeing him from a distance, Shaun concluded that he would have to do whatever it took to protect himself. This was his 'hinge moment'. Right from the start he wanted to be someone who didn't just merge with the crowd or go with the flow. He had decided from that moment that he was going to be the hardest boy at school. It was just a state of mind, he reckoned. No one would mess with him.

He was right. Being bigger than average certainly helped. Within weeks he was in the company of Mark – one of the toughest bullies at Regent's High, and none of their behaviour went unnoticed. Their reputation preceded them wherever they went. Pupils went out of their way to avoid their gaze, especially in situations like riding the school bus when there was no authority figure to save them. Every teacher knew the names 'Shaun and Mark' and many were looking for ways to rid their classes of them.

After just a few weeks the two boys were sent to the isolation room because of their constant fighting. This didn't bother Shaun. The fact that they were in this room proved that they were as tough as everyone thought. Anyway, as far as Shaun was concerned, he needed to keep being associated with Mark. That way he was untouchable. No one would ever mess with Mark. He was from a rough estate, he smoked weed, he could bully for Britain, and he'd mentor Shaun into the tough lad he desired to be.

It wasn't long before the head of year was requesting the presence of Shaun's parents almost every evening to talk about his behaviour that day. When they returned from the meetings, Shaun would quietly observe the emotional strain on his Mum's face and the look of permanent shock that his Dad carried. One evening, Shaun's Dad was driving him home after yet another fight and a string of detentions. It was a miracle that he hadn't been suspended. His Dad hadn't said much to him about his behaviour because nothing seemed to make a difference. All the members of the family had done their fair share of shouting at Shaun, but all comment over the last two years had gone in one ear and out the other. Tonight was different. It was only a few words, but Shaun can remember them as clearly as if they were spoken yesterday: 'I'm really disappointed in you, son.' The comment nailed Shaun to his car seat and dominated his every moment for the rest of the journey.

The minute they arrived home Shaun was sent to his room. With nothing much to do, he flung himself down on his bed, sharing the space with magazines and chocolate wrappers. Closing his eyes helped to remove him from the shame of what he had just experienced. Why was he suddenly caring about what his Dad thought? From nowhere a picture flashed into his head. He could clearly see his Dad cradling him in his arms as a tiny baby. He had such a loving expression on his face. Shaun knew instantly that his Dad had stood there believing that his precious son was going to make him a proud father. As he gazed at the picture, Shaun was somehow reminded that this was how God felt about him too. God cared for him and God also wanted to be a proud Father. In that moment,

Shaun knew that he wanted to change. It shocked him that he was even thinking about God at all. He thought he'd left that stuff behind at primary school. He couldn't believe he was doing it, but out of his mouth spilled the first prayer he'd prayed in years: 'Lord, please help me to be better.'

There was no overnight change, but Shaun knew that his Dad's words were a turning-point. They hit him so hard that he had decided that he didn't want to let his Dad down any more. The tough exterior that he was carrying around was just that: an exterior. If Mark and the other kids at school could see inside him (and he wasn't sure he wanted them to) they would realize that there was more. So far his stubbornness had won the day and he had chosen to go against everything his family wanted, but that was because his head had been dictating everything. Now something different was happening to him; his heart was speaking up as well.

Slowly his lifestyle began to change. It was tough revealing a new side to himself at school, but he was determined to do it. He gradually stopped hanging around with Mark and his mates, and adopted a new group of friends. He got a hard time for his change in loyalty but his stubbornness again prevented him from backing down. Ironically, Mark began to show Shaun some respect as time passed by. He couldn't get to grips with why he would no longer use violence to protect himself or maintain some sort of popularity. It was weird that he would no longer hook up with any girl around, smoke weed on the school bus, or drink copious amounts of alcohol round at his house. In actual fact, although Mark wouldn't admit it to anyone, the new Shaun intrigued him.

Shaun had hooked up with a local Anglican church, where he was encouraged to get involved in working with other young people. He was surprised to find that he had something to offer them. He started helping out at the kids' club and found that he felt at home working with some of the toughest lads in Bootle. He was drawn to the ones who swore all the time and fought with each other. The youth leaders were keen to see Shaun grow in his faith, so they involved him in various new activities. He was invited to help DJ at a Christian event, and although he had never before even put a needle anywhere near a piece of vinyl, he said yes. He loved music and his natural confidence convinced him he could pull it off.

It was a real success. People seemed to connect with the music he played, and the experience reminded him of a Youth For Christ team called Activate who had come into his school two or three years previously. They had spent a week taking assemblies and lessons, performing drama, dance and music, and talking about God. The members of the team and their message had really made an impression on him at the time. Some of their stock phrases about God's love were still lodged in his head.

As Shaun neared the end of his time at school, his passion and heart for other young people were increasing by the day. He wondered if he should get involved in work like Activate's. A team like that would be a place where he could really get to grips with his gifts and work out exactly what he had to offer. He didn't think he had a chance of getting into Activate, but then he heard that his cousin had been accepted. Shaun thought, 'If he can do it, then so can I!'

Now here he was, halfway through his gap year with Activate, beginning to fully understand that his calling was to work with lost, rough young guys. When people used the word 'deprived' to talk about their area, he knew exactly what the kids had been deprived of. Love. He knew the black holes in their family relationships, and felt that he could be a male role model to them. He looked around the drop-in centre, refocusing on the rowdy rough and tumble at his feet. He'd had some great conversations with some of the lads recently and loved simply being there for them, answering their questions about life, the universe and everything. He had even had a chance to talk to some of them about Jesus. He felt as if he really had something to offer them. 'Boy, my life has changed!' he observed.

Later that week, Shaun joined the rest of the gap-year volunteers for some time out to think about the future. A presentation was made about YFC's work in prisons, engaging with lads via music, theatre and rap workshops. His attention was immediately drawn. Later that day a YFC staff member suggested to him that he would be perfect for working on the prisons team. He didn't know whether it was right for him, but the more he thought about it, the more it made sense. He remembered a book his Grandad had given him called *God's Prison Gang*. He had been fascinated by prison and within days had gobbled up this story of people finding faith behind bars. He was reminded of how he had felt when he had put the book down. He had said to himself, 'Even if I don't end up there myself, I want to give money to prisons work in the future.' He knew it could be challenging, but what an opportunity it would be to help guys who were really struggling.

His fellow members of Activate kept telling him that he would be a really great prisons worker, able to connect with the prisoners on their level. He wasn't sure if this was a compliment, but deep down he knew they might be right. He was also reminded of the fact that for many years his Grandad had been faithfully working for Jesus in the prison around the corner from his house. It began to seem obvious to Shaun that his skills in working with difficult and deprived lads would be best used in the environment of a young offenders' institution. The door opened wide, and a couple of months later he joined YFC's prisons team.

His first assignment was working in prisons in the North-West of England. On arrival he was pleased to find that many of the inmates were Scousers – having the same language really helped him to connect with them quickly. He laughed on his first day as he recalled a time when he was being a particularly naughty boy, causing his Mum to shout, 'You're going to end up in prison! Your Grandad will be visiting you one day in there!' The irony was that here he was, but not as an inmate. He was there serving Jesus with all his heart, and he felt at home. It made Shaun reflect on his past and be thankful. His Dad's words had changed everything. No longer were the words 'I'm really disappointed in you, son' ringing in his ears, as his Dad had recently told him how proud he was of the life he was now living. This had made Shaun so happy. Yes, his primary calling was to serve God, but his Dad's affirmation and support gave him even greater encouragement and assurance that he was doing the right thing. Shaun was so glad that he had changed the course of his life – especially when he came face to face with lads from Mark's gang who were now behind bars. Things could have been so different.

Part of the prison team's weekly programme involved performing two short plays. In one he was a tough lad and in the other he was a prisoner. The inmates could somehow see themselves in Shaun, and he could see himself in them, creating a mutual respect that opened doors for him to share Jesus.

He continues to have loads of opportunities to chat with lads about

God and to pray with them in their cells. Shaun was able to pray with a lad who had injured his back. Three other prisoners joined in the prayer, and the next day his back was fine. Simple steps of faith are being taken. Whether Shaun is sharing his story, acting, or just chatting, God uses him to powerfully touch inmates' lives.

Just recently Shaun was given the job of leading YFC's 'Inside Out' prisons team. So there will be many more days of performing, praying – and probably getting beaten on a Playstation!

Sadly, Shaun's Grandad has become too frail to continue his prison work. Shaun feels that the baton is being passed to him and that God is saying, 'I want prison ministry to continue in this family, and you're the one to take it on.' It's as if someone else's game is over, but he's been passed the control pad. The screen ahead of him is begging the question, 'Continue?'

Dancing on Sand, Walking on Water

> During the fourth watch of the night Jesus went out to them, walking on the lake. When the disciples saw him walking on the lake, they were terrified. 'It's a ghost,' they said, and cried out in fear.
>
> But Jesus immediately said to them: 'Take courage! It is I. Don't be afraid.'
>
> 'Lord, if it's you,' Peter replied, 'tell me to come to you on the water.'
>
> 'Come,' he said.
>
> Then Peter got down out of the boat, walked on the water and came towards Jesus. But when he saw the wind, he was afraid and, beginning to sink, cried out, 'Lord, save me!'
>
> Immediately Jesus reached out his hand and caught him. 'You of little faith,' he said, 'why did you doubt?'
>
> And when they climbed into the boat, the wind died down. Then those who were in the boat worshipped him, saying, 'Truly you are the Son of God.'   (Matthew 14:25–33)

I saw something beautiful recently while sitting on an inner-city beach in Chicago. A father was playing with his son. There was much tickling and running around, with continual yelps of extreme pleasure coming from the little man, who couldn't have been anything more than four years old. Then something happened that made the child stop dead in his sandy little tracks. There was an unexpected hiatus of silence. He was staring at his father in total surprise, because Dad looked like he had never looked before. His feet were where his hands should have been and his arms were where his legs should have been. Now he was even walking around, looking like some sort of alien.

As a secretive observer from a distance, I was at first simply impressed by this father's gymnastic ability, but I was unprepared for the beauty of what happened next. The son started trying to do what he had seen his father doing. I don't know if you have ever seen a four-year-old attempt a handstand, but it's a pretty comedic event. Much minor sandstorm and crying ensued before Dad came to the rescue.

And then before me was a phenomenal picture. A loving father stooped over his young son, tenderly holding his feet steady, so that he could do a handstand like his Dad. The smile returned. It returned with such vengeance that I immediately forgot the time during which it had been absent. It made me think that all our attempts to do what we see the Father doing must look equally laughable when we try to make it happen on our own. I think Peter would agree with me on that one. How often do we let God hold our feet?

So much has been written about these magical moments when Peter walked on water. Perhaps that is because we easily identify with these moments as a microcosm of our own journeys with Jesus. Peter went from excited to victorious, to floating, to floundering, to sinking, to being in need of rescue. Do any of those stages sound familiar? They are certainly familiar to young people like Rebecca. Peter goes through practically every physical and emotional state that we may cycle through in a year, in the space of just a minute!

You see, I think we often forget that the sea is in fact still the sea. As Peter took those first tentative steps across the Sea of Galilee, he wasn't surfing something that had suddenly ceased to be liquid. My mind goes back to one of Spiderman's superhero sidekicks called Ice-man, who surfed along on the ice he created, a stylish shuffle of his wrists producing a hand-drier in reverse. I don't think Jesus was pulling that kind of stunt.

There is a crucial mistake we can so easily make during the mountain-top experiences of our Christian lives. It is believing that because we are enjoying this moment in this place at this time, and because we are in wonderful communion with our God, the world has ceased to be the choppy, swirling, confusing, evil-laden place that it still is. I think the devil loves to fool us into expecting a new heaven and a new earth right now, so he can get us complaining when we discover that it didn't arrive while we were at the summit. That day will come – and boy, are we looking forward to the absence of sin and suffering – but it's not here yet, and if the TV news channels are anything to go by, then we're still some distance from that point.

It's inevitable that we will come down to earth with a bump if we've been forgetting to keep our feet on the ground while our head is in the clouds. I've seen it happen to so many young Christians, as the stories in this book vividly illustrate. Helen and Rebecca both struggled to understand how a good God could have allowed their respective situations to become as bad as they did.

When playing cards, we understand that sometimes we'll get high cards and sometimes we'll get low ones. It doesn't stop us complaining, but we mostly accept the situation. Yet in life, I fear we have a belief in God as a cosmic magician who will only deal us high cards, having magically removed all the low ones from the deck. High cards can only *be* high cards if there are low cards in there too. Conversely, do we let him hold our feet when we're holding a good hand?

The two storms that Peter experienced with Jesus were vital to the development of his faith. In many ways he had to sink so that he could take the next step in his faith journey. The little guy in Chicago had to eat a few sand sandwiches before he could realize his need of his father. You can see the progression in Peter's faith from 'Who is this man?' during storm 1 (Matthew 8) to 'Truly, you are the Son of God' during storm 2 (Matthew 14). Similarly, the storms that

Helen and Rebecca experienced have been crucial to their spiritual formation, but they've only seen that with the benefit of hindsight. Self-sufficiency is a curse of this generation, and you only learn the important lesson that you're not self-sufficient when you get that sinking feeling. However, many of us never experience that sinking feeling because there's only so far you can sink if you're still on the sand.

Therefore, in my work with Youth For Christ, I often tell the story of the two balloonists who were the first to travel all the way around the world in a hot-air balloon. It was a huge silver balloon called the Breitling Orbiter. In honesty, I was first attracted to their story because they had beaten Richard Branson. (Call me twisted, but I kind of just enjoyed that fact!) They just about made it to the finish line, having had many near-death experiences. On various occasions they were powerless and at the mercy of the Atlantic's unpredictable weather patterns, and could only wait, hope and pray, with very little water and oxygen.

I watched an interview with the two men on their return, and in it they talked at length about how they had not realized exactly how dangerous and scary the trip would be. They freely admitted that they had never done anything so crazy and risky in all their lives. As they talked about their (quite literally) up-and-down journey, I couldn't help thinking that their experience was a remarkable parable for the adventure of knowing God.

They spoke of how they didn't really know what they were letting themselves in for (I think Peter could nod his head to that one). They spoke of how flying so far above the earth totally changed their perspective on life – they had more of a sense of awe, wonder and gratitude (I sense Peter nodding again). And they talked of how the only thing that really got them through was the strength of their relationship. Without that they would have spiralled into despair (I don't think we even need to ask Peter how important a certain relationship was). All in all, they summed it up by saying that it was risky, scary and a little bit crazy, but when asked if they regretted it, there was no discussion. 'Not for a second,' came their reply.

So, almost every time I speak to a group of young people, I make a point of stressing that yes, what I am describing to them is certainly not the easiest life possible, but it is definitely the best life possible. As the years have gone by in my life, I say it with increasing sincerity. My life has got better and better but also harder and harder. And I don't regret the adventure for a second.

Positive vibes

The passage also highlights beautifully the tensions at play when young people are stepping out in faith for God. Yes, there is often no shortage of enthusiasm. Yes, there is often a quickly raised hand to volunteer. Yes, there is much trumpeting of the valiant act. But there are also often those moments of blind panic when the safety-net has been taken away, there's no one else to cling to and you feel like you're falling fast. Yet again, I feel the challenge to be there in the storm, as Jesus was, for one of these young people who are splashing around desperately.

I can imagine Jesus' words on their return to the boat: 'I know you trust me, or you wouldn't have got out of the boat in the first place, but why didn't you trust yourself?' 'Why did you doubt that you could keep going?' I can imagine him quoting Paul (even though Paul hasn't written these words yet!):

he who began a good work in you will carry it on to completion.

(Philippians 1:6)

Then I realize that perhaps I am projecting my critical twenty-first-century mind-set onto Jesus. On further reflection, I wonder if Jesus has already said all he needs to say along those lines while he was standing on the water. His words, once back in the boat, would surely have been more like, 'Well done, Peter. You had faith in me. You stepped out in faith beyond your human abilities, knowing that you needed my power to make it work. I didn't see any of the others leaping at the opportunity. It has been wet, public and at times hilarious, but you have grown today.'

How often, like Matthew, are we quite efficient at reporting what has gone wrong when, for example, young people have planned and executed an event, but slow to congratulate or encourage? I will always be gagging to mention three or four teaching points in my critique of a song or sermon, but only through discipline and clenched teeth do I manage to remember to applaud what has been good. Our reaction to the early efforts of young people could well make all the difference to whether or not there are any further efforts at all. Active encouragement creates a forum for active discipleship. Too often we avoid both by making no comment at all.

There were two people in particular who encouraged me to keep going when they saw the spark of something good amidst the nonsense of my teenage ego. Their names were Billy Blair and Stephen Forde. Both of them in different contexts continually encouraged me to keep using music to communicate and to lead others in worship, even when many of my experiments went none too well. There were many times when I failed to involve others as I should have, times when I didn't serve the bigger purpose, and times when, quite simply, my guitar wasn't even close to being in tune, but still these guys encouraged me to keep going, to keep walking. You see, any young person sticking their neck out to lead is in a pretty exposed position, much like Peter on the water. It's very easy for the fear to kick in when, for example, confronted with a congregation of 150 people, many of whom aren't smiling back at you. We've got to be close enough to grab the young people's hands when they start to sink. The importance of this is multiplied by the cynical context in which young people exist. Negativity and criticism are the mother tongues of the playground, so you would not believe what an impact even the smallest of positive words can make. They are the surprising sirens that create forward momentum in a life, cutting through the gridlock of despondency. Building young people up is a vital discipline. And eventually they understand that the only reason why you also make critical suggestions is that you believe there is something worthwhile in them that is worth working on.

I have experienced helpful criticism myself. I had been at secondary school for a couple of years, but my sister Ruth (who is three years younger than me) was still at primary school. I was being a dutiful brother and joining our Mum at Ruth's school concert. Ruth was playing flute in the orchestra, which I had proudly been the leader of two years previously (I still have the shield to prove it!). The problem was that I was struggling to sit through the orchestra's rendition of some barely recognizable piece by Beethoven. The strings were woefully out of tune, the brass section kept arriving before they were invited, and the young guy on percussion obviously just enjoyed hitting things (he had only one volume level – monstrous). I whispered my discomfort to my mother, who turned with a smile and said, 'Well, they're three times better than you lot were!' My jaw dropped to the floor. A metaphorical carpet had been pulled out from under me. What?! We were worse than that?! Shame flooded over me. Why did no one ever tell us? Eventually someone did tell me a few months later. His name was Mr Short and he was my violin teacher. It was like a gutless boy splitting up with a girl. 'It's just not working out, Andrew, is it?' he said. It was the release I needed to pass on my violin to a much worthier recipient and grab a guitar. I'm so glad I did.

Sent

I wonder to what extent Peter and the disciples realized that Jesus' intention for them was to be sent out without him. They were enjoying being in the presence of the hottest ticket in town, as he toured around preaching and healing. There was serious kudos from even being in his vicinity. Sure, Peter was drinking it all in, becoming more like his Master, but did he ever think he would hear these words?

> As you go, preach this message: 'The kingdom of heaven is near.' Heal the sick, raise the dead, cleanse those who have leprosy, drive out demons. Freely you have received, freely give. (Matthew 10:7–8)

Peter may well have thought, 'Hang on, Jesus. You never said anything about us doing this on our own. I thought we were going to change the world, with you at the front of the battle, and us following in your wake!' If all that wasn't scary enough, then look what comes next:

> Do not take along any gold or silver or copper in your belts; take no bag for the journey, or extra tunic, or sandals or a staff; for the worker is worth his keep. (Matthew 10:9–10)

Suddenly they realize that they aren't going to be able to bluff this one. This is going to take some real faith. Their whole understanding of what this adventure is about has shifted forever.

I love watching Youth For Christ team members speak in school assemblies for the first time. Usually that role is fulfilled by a team leader who has plenty of experience in public speaking. But at some stage of the year the team leader will throw someone in at the deep end to do the talking. There is excitement and extreme fear, as an eighteen- or nineteen-year-old gets ready to talk to perhaps 500 young people, only slightly younger than they are. Much prayer is directed upward and powerful communication usually happens, just as in Jemima's first assembly. Even when folks 'bottle it', their transparency and honesty enable them to connect with those standing in front of them. The gathered crowd know that this is a real person, and not a slick automaton trying to sell them something. Folks who have been thrown in at the deep end often report that they learnt more in the minutes of doing the talk than in the days of training beforehand. It's only when you're standing there that you realize the dynamics involved in a situation like that – whether it's making yourself heard, maintaining discipline, not offending the staff, finishing well or any number of other factors. It's only in the midst of this battle that you realize how useful your training has been, and that you still need more training, as you're not quite there yet! Before you're dropped into a real-life scenario, it's easy to wrongly think that you're already the finished article.

Jesus is the great teacher, and great teachers know when they should step aside and allow folks to experience for themselves what they've been learning about. People must make their own mistakes and learn their own lessons. People need to move from being spectators to being participants. This is learning that lasts. I don't know how much French you can still speak. I enjoyed learning French at school, but the French phrases that I can still use today are those that I used in the villages and campsites of Brittany and the Vendee during family holidays. At those times my small amount of classroom knowledge had to hit the ground running. Through curious looks from shop-owners I learnt what worked and what didn't and so I got better, but most importantly, I can still remember those phrases now. I'm not saying that my classroom foundation wasn't important, but without putting what I had learnt into practice, it would have remained useless and atrophied, as much of my unpractised vocabulary did.

Jesus, the Master, was sending out his apprentices on the first ever gap year (or perhaps it was only a few weeks), and it was really important that he wasn't there (in a manner of speaking)! For as long as they could rely on him to 'do the business', they would never develop their own gifts. Lewis and Shaun both have bosses at YFC (I know them) who can preach, teach and interact better than they can, but I know that when they receive a request to go and speak somewhere, it's in their DNA to think, 'Would it be better to send one of the new guys, like Lewis or Shaun?' Yes, the event might be 'better' if they went and did it themselves, but the long-term upside for the kingdom is larger if they don't. Jesus understood multiplication and exponential growth.

Hospitality

As well as being scared by the overall concept of being sent out without Jesus, some of the specifics of his instructions may well have freaked out the disciples. He told them not to take any cash or plastic. They may have wondered how they would survive. Jesus assured them that they would be looked after and would enjoy hospitality (but not from everyone). They really were going to be living by faith and not by Judas' budget. YFC staff and volunteers often face this challenge. They need to raise funding from friends, family and supporting churches. To a young person this can seem like a daunting task. In our self-sufficient society, we have been trained to believe that asking for anything is a sign of weakness, even though Jesus makes it clear that 'the worker deserves his wages' (Luke 10:7). We are actually giving people a chance to be blessed, by allowing them to give. Even while typing that last sentence, I am fighting my worldly perception to believe that it is true. You don't have to be a genius to work out that Western society's attitude to money is the root cause of so many problems, and intentional giving to support counter-cultural activity is a fantastic way of subverting the status quo. It's always a challenge for YFC staff to raise 50 per cent of their salaries from personal supporters, but when they look back, everyone reports what a healthy, humbling process it is. The discipline of the process keeps you grounded and helps you to realize whose shoulders you are standing on. This direct link is much better than an assumption that the money you are paid simply comes from some magic porridge pot that is always running over.

Another positive is that generally, when people have a financial stake in you, they also pray more diligently for you.

For many of us, accepting or giving hospitality can be a challenge. Again, this form of giving is very counter-cultural, and we can feel that we have lost control when we have strangers in our houses, or vice versa! The disciples were sacrificing the comfort and sense of belonging of their own homes and families to depend on the hospitality (or not) of strangers. I could tell you many funny stories of YFC volunteers coping (or not) with staying in strangers' houses. There have been wonderful moments, such as children of the family becoming Christians around the dinner table, or emotionally distant fathers returning to their sons because 'God was in the air'. There have also been comedy moments when vans have ploughed up beautiful lawns, or baths have been left running for a little too long! It all adds to the organic, messy, living, breathing thing that is the kingdom of God. Instead of sanitized, organized 'keeping oneself to oneself', there is sharing, caring and fellowship.

Healing?

Another thing in Jesus' commissioning speech that, I think, may have made the disciples' ears prick up, was this: 'Heal the sick...'

I used to work as a hospital doctor, and if Jesus was giving the staff a motivational speech first thing every morning, I think I could cope with it. When you work in a hospital, 'Heal the sick' doesn't sound impossible as a mission statement for the day. But what if Jesus turned up at your place of work and gave you the 'Heal the sick' speech? How would you feel? Scared? Inadequate? Reaching for a First Aid kit? That's not too dissimilar to what happened to the disciples. As far as we know, they hadn't 'done' any healing yet. Sure, they'd seen Jesus in action, but he was the Son of God, so he was special. That sort of stuff wasn't really an option for them, was it?

Let me tell you a story about two Scottish girls. Jennifer met Sarah only once, but both their stories were forever altered by their encounter. Jennifer was seventeen. Sarah was nineteen. Jennifer, in her own words, was 'brought up quite rough'. Her father left home when she was young, and she now had two half-sisters as well as her two brothers. Many of her family were deeply enmeshed in witchcraft. Aged nine, she was diagnosed with epilepsy, and since that time she had been having seizures at unpredictable moments, which left her embarrassed and lacking in confidence. She was bullied all the way through her school life because people saw her as different.

Sarah was on a gap-year programme with Youth For Christ. She had been a Christian since she was four years old, and had always been encouraged to pray for people. She began to notice that sometimes when she prayed for people, they got better. She simply assumed that that was what happened every time anyone prayed. It was a simple faith that prayer worked. The girls met when Sarah was working on the merchandise stall at a Kurios gig (Kurios are YFC's band in Scotland). There were about fifty young people present, and towards the end of the concert one of the band members said that if anyone wanted to be prayed for, they would be more than happy to pray with them. There was hardly anyone left in the hall by the time Jennifer walked towards Sarah. She hadn't been sure whether or not to ask someone to pray, as she'd been ill for so long. However, a recent increase in her symptoms meant that she had a brain scan coming up the next day, so she thought, 'What harm can it do?'

Sarah listened to Jennifer's story and shared some Bible verses with her before laying her hands on her and praying for her. She prayed very specifically, 'God, would you take away the epilepsy? Would you not just remove the symptoms? Would you remove it completely? We want tomorrow's scan to be completely clear.'

I won't stretch out the story for the sake of it. The scan was completely clear. The results came through a couple of weeks later, and Jennifer emailed the band to let them know. A year later, there is still no sign of the epilepsy. She has been completely healed. When I asked her what difference this has made to her life, she said, 'A BIG difference. I am so happy now. It has changed so much in me. If you knew me as well as some people know me, you would be able to see the difference.' Wow!

If you got to know Sarah, you'd find that she is a lovely, unassuming young woman. No flashy words, no big ego – just a faith that when Jesus says, 'Go, heal the sick...' he means it. It's still happening!

Fly or die

When I read of the disciples being sent out on a limb, I can't help thinking about the peregrine falcons I had the privilege of seeing near Ross-on-Wye last year. Peregrine falcons are the fastest-moving creatures in the world. They can fly at up to 200 miles per hour. We looked at these beautiful birds' nests through telescopes. They were stuck in the smallest of crevices high up in the cliffs, hundreds of feet above the ground. I wondered how on earth they could teach their young to fly so fast with so little space. The RSPB expert standing beside me chuckled. 'Ah, that's easy,' he said. 'They just boot them out.' After my initial shock he went on to explain how, even though they've only ever seen brief moments of their parents' flights through a thin crack, the falcon chicks just get nudged off the ledge! I couldn't believe it. He explained that it's not the same story with eagles, who drop their young, then scoop them up again if they're struggling. Hence this verse in Exodus:

> You yourselves have seen what I did to Egypt, and how I carried you on eagles' wings and brought you to myself. (Exodus 19:4)

The young falcons basically have two options – fly or die. Talk about survival of the fittest! I am so glad that Jesus wasn't sending the disciples out unprepared, and without his power, but that he simply did push them out, whether they liked it or not. I'm glad that that's what happened to Lewis, Shaun, Sarah and Jemima too. I'm glad that YFC pushed them out into the real world, whether they thought they were ready or not. Otherwise they may never have flown like they have.

Foot in mouth (1)

This whole empowerment thing always sounds good in theory and we happily murmur our agreement. But what happens when the church hall has been trashed, and the talk we delegated was meaningless, bordering on blasphemous? I believe we lose track of the fact that Peter and the disciples were not, as we might put it, 'sorted'. In fact they weren't even close to 'sorted'. They were still asking Jesus questions that would make your eyes roll. They must have been thinking, 'How can we explain the good news of the kingdom when we're not really sure what or where it is?' Peter especially must have been incredulous that he was going to have the task of telling God's story, because every time he asked something or did something, he seemed to get it wrong. He felt like he was at the bottom of the class. Two classic examples of this occurred just six days apart, as told in Mark's Gospel:

> He then began to teach them that the Son of Man must suffer many things and be rejected by the elders, chief priests and teachers of the law, and that he must be killed and after three days rise again. He spoke plainly about this, and Peter took him aside and began to rebuke him.
>
> But when Jesus turned and looked at his disciples, he rebuked Peter.

'Get behind me, Satan!' he said. 'You do not have in mind the things of God, but the things of men.'

(Mark 8:31–33)

It's half-time in the World Cup Final. You're playing for England and you're 1–0 up against Argentina. You take your seat in the dressing-room, and the manager begins his half-time team talk. So far the team's tactics have been faultless. His words are inspiring. You agree with what he's saying and a patriotic desire to win for your country is rising up inside you. The manager is the right man in the right place at the right time. This is the moment you've been waiting for all your life. This is the moment when all the hard work will be worth it.

But then the manager drops a bombshell. He's resigning. What?! Not now! Not when things have been going so well! We're on the brink of a great victory, and he's disappearing! You speak up to say what everyone else must be thinking too: 'No way, boss! You're not leaving!'

The manager turns towards you and accuses you of being the Argentinian manager. He's saying that your loyalties lie with the other team. Your patriotic bubble is burst in a very public way. You slam your boots into the floor and walk out. 'What could he be thinking? What is going on here that I don't understand? Why would he accuse me of being in league with the other side?' It hurts.

That story may seem extraordinary, but it is no more extraordinary than what happened to Peter when he tried to express his loyalty to Jesus. Instead of a friendly, 'Thanks, mate. It's nice to know you're on my side', he got a verbal volley that he could never have expected. However, if we look more closely we can see why it came his way. Jesus had been taking some time to explain what was coming for him. He wasn't trying to protect the disciples from the truth. He was being increasingly specific about his death and resurrection. Verse 32 says, 'he spoke plainly about this'.

Yet this had all floated above Peter's head, as he was still seeing Jesus through the lens of *his* expectations. In the mental story that Peter was writing, there was no place for death, only huge popularity and the crowning of a new king and his loyal advisers. Jesus knows the origin of the force that would attempt to steer him away from his mission towards triumphant earthly power, so he names him. Satan.

Do we spend our time yearning for the logistics of our lives to be easier? Are we yearning for the structural problems to be sorted? Or are we crying out for God's agenda, for his kingdom to come, no matter how messy that may look? Are we desperate for our young people to be more polite, rather than sold out for God? Would we rather they got 'a good education' instead of following where he leads? Are we sometimes looking at young people through the lens of our expectations rather than God's? How often can it be said of us that 'You do not have in mind the things of God, but the things of men'?

Sometimes it is hard to see the big picture. When we are intensely involved in any relationship, it is often difficult to see where that relationship fits into the big story of God. As we see from Shaun's story, his life gained a new impetus and direction when he realized that his grandfather had blazed a trail for him. He recognized that he was stepping into the shoes of some powerful family heritage and he was stronger for it. We often make the mistake of inviting God into our story. We know our story well. It's what we can control. We get an idea of what we would like to have in it, and we ask God to bless it. Our tunnel vision and selfish ambition kick in so easily if we walk and pray through life this way. What if, instead of asking God to be involved in our story, we asked him how we could be involved in his story? Shaun knew that God was moving in the young offenders' institutions of the UK and he wanted to lend his shoulder to what was going on. Our perception of ourselves makes all the difference. Do we see ourselves as superstars for the kingdom, whom God is lucky to have on his side? Or are we willing servants who are ready to play their part, eagerly awaiting direction from the great Playwright?

Peter's shock would have been all the larger as, earlier in this very chapter, he had correctly identified Jesus as the Christ. Obviously those words meant something different to him than they did to Jesus. Perhaps they needed another chat, he thought. But maybe after everyone had cooled down a bit.

Foot in mouth (2)

It was six days later. The respectable cooling off period was over. Jesus hand-picked Peter, James and John to go hiking with him. Peter hadn't a clue what was going on, but he was very relieved to find that his recent *faux-pas* didn't seem to have counted against him. It felt good that he was back in his rightful place in Jesus' inner sanctum. Little did he realize the magnitude of what was about to happen:

> After six days Jesus took Peter, James and John with him and led them up a high mountain, where they were all alone. There he was transfigured before them. His clothes became dazzling white, whiter than anyone in the world could bleach them. And there appeared before them Elijah and Moses, who were talking with Jesus.
>
> Peter said to Jesus, 'Rabbi, it is good for us to be here. Let us put up three shelters – one for you, one for Moses and one for Elijah.' (He did not know what to say, they were so frightened.)
>
> Then a cloud appeared and enveloped them, and a voice came from the cloud: 'This is my Son, whom I love. Listen to him!'
>
> Suddenly, when they looked round, they no longer saw anyone with them except Jesus.
>
> As they were coming down the mountain, Jesus gave them orders not to tell anyone what they had seen until the Son of Man had risen from the dead. They kept the matter to themselves, discussing what 'rising from the dead' meant. (Mark 9:2–10)

Surely this is the definitive 'mountain-top experience' with Jesus. Peter probably thought it couldn't get any better than this. Jesus was pulling back the veil from his eyes to enable him to see just a smidgeon of his glory. The multi-media extravaganza must have been pretty impressive to a first-century man. Booming voices, bright lights, and two old stars making a dramatic comeback! Especially when those two were none other than Moses and Elijah. It was heaven on earth for a Jewish man. He was sharing the stage with some big hitters, even though one does wonder how he recognized them without ever having seen them on TV!

Right now, stop and think about who you would most like to meet. Who has most motivated and inspired you? They can be from any time or place. They can be from any sphere of society – medical, sporting, religious, whatever... It might be Nelson Mandela, Mother Teresa, or William Wilberforce. Imagine if their entourages are nowhere to be seen and it's just you and them. You get to ask all the questions you've always wanted to. You get to simply be where they are for a few moments. There is an indescribable electricity involved in moments like that. Now multiply that by a factor of ten thousand, and you probably still won't get close to what it felt like for the disciples to be on the top of that mountain.

If you've had an earthly moment like that, how did you feel? Were you coherent when you spoke, or did your nerves get the better of you? Peter fell into the trap that so many of us fall into when confronted with absolute majesty, power and authority. He felt the need to say something. We can't seem to cope with silence. I remember being at the wedding party of a famous politician and, when I was introduced to him, I said something utterly facile like, 'The walls of this room are nice, aren't they?' That sort of stuff just comes out of us when we are overcome by a situation or a person. You then spend the next half-hour chanting, 'Why did I say that?', rehearsing the moment again and again in your head, but by that time, it's too late. So I can totally identify with Peter here. As ever, he was thinking, 'Well, somebody has to say something', bravely taking the responsibility onto his fragile shoulders. What he came up with was certainly creative and functional, but, as ever, he gloriously missed the point. He was scared stiff, but aware that he was sharing in a privileged moment that he wanted to last for longer than just a moment. He suggested building three shelters for the three dignitaries. He was thinking, 'Let's turn this one-night-only performance into a long-running Broadway spectacle.' He was mentally working out where to put the seats and what price the interval ice creams should be, when he realized that no one else was paying any attention to his idea. Or maybe he thought Jesus wanted to start his own Christian festival. (So Easter and Christmas aren't good enough?) I worry about the amount of energy we put into 'housing' our mountain-top experiences with God. We build fancy buildings, pay for top-of-the-range sound systems, and generally create environments that are conducive to sucking people in, rather than sending them out again. It is so easy to institutionalize a move of God. It becomes a seven-step programme, a trendy T-shirt or a range of books with matching DVDs. Jesus knew that they weren't going to be hanging around on this mountain-top. Important revelation had been shared, but the work was now going to be continued down on lower ground. There was no direct rebuke for Peter this time, just the realization that he was out of his depth. As Matthew's account records:

> While he was still speaking, a bright cloud enveloped them, and a voice from the cloud said, 'This is my Son, whom I love; with him I am well pleased. Listen to him!' (Matthew 17:5)

That was pretty polite, really. I think Peter got the idea that he should stop talking:

> When the disciples heard this, they fell face down to the ground, terrified. But Jesus came and touched them. 'Get up,' he said. 'Don't be afraid.'

To be fair to Peter, there was some context for his suggestion. The feast of booths involved the setting up of such shelters, and the Israelites had been used to pitching the tabernacle to hold God's presence. Perhaps he knew that he could not continue to be in the presence of this glory and stay alive, so these shelters were meant as an act of self-preservation. But God himself provided the protection as a bright cloud enveloped them.

Bottom of the class

So in light of all Peter's failed attempts to do the right thing, we can only imagine what he was thinking when Jesus sent him out to be his messenger. We know that Peter would have had no shortage of enthusiasm, but there was no way that Jesus could have believed that Peter had passed his theological exit exams with flying colours.

Here is the point where we need to ask ourselves some serious questions about those whom we share our lives with. Are we holding them in the classroom when they need to be getting on 'with their Father's business'? The journey of Jesus and Peter gives us a very good measure of where Jesus' tolerance levels were in terms of trust and releasing ministry, and of his acceptance of far from fully formed theology in the heads and hearts of his messengers.

What was unmistakably there was a relationship. Peter's relationship with Jesus had become the centrepiece of his life. It was the filter through which all other considerations were passed – where he went, what he said, and how he thought. Everything returned to this axis of trust. He loved this man who had invaded his life and asked him to follow him. He could do nothing else, even if the closeness with which he followed at times led him into embarrassment or ridicule.

This is the sort of relationship that I see in the lives of people like Tim and Steve. They saw what, to most of us, would have been only a tragic and frustrating situation through the lens of their relationship with Jesus, and realized it was an opportunity. The love that Jemima was experiencing from being in relationship with this same Jesus changed all her attitudes to herself and her potential. She began to see how she was gifted and had the security to point out others' gifts too.

On the tip of my tongue

When poked with many questions on that stationary train, Tim's open and honest confession of his Saviour has echoes of Peter answering a very important question from Jesus:

> When Jesus came to the region of Caesarea Philippi, he asked his disciples, 'Who do people say the Son of Man is?'
>
> They replied, 'Some say John the Baptist; others say Elijah; and still others, Jeremiah or one of the prophets.'
>
> 'But what about you?' he asked. 'Who do you say I am?'
>
> Simon Peter answered, 'You are the Christ, the Son of the living God.'
>
> Jesus replied, 'Blessed are you, Simon son of Jonah, for this was not revealed to you by man, but by my Father in heaven. And I tell you that you are Peter, and on this rock I will build my church, and the gates of Hades will not overcome it. I will give you the keys of the kingdom of heaven; whatever you bind on earth will be bound in heaven, and whatever you loose on earth will be loosed in heaven.' (Matthew 16:13–19)

We have seen Peter's enthusiasm get him into trouble, but this is surely a moment where we can celebrate his famous boldness. Jesus had asked the most important question in the world. Whether we like it or not, as our post-modern world debates endless questions in wall-to-wall talk shows and radio phone-ins, Jesus' question is still the most important. Do we really believe that?

'Who do you say that I am?' How someone answers that question goes a long way to determining where they will spend eternity and what they will spend it doing, and I struggle to see how any current issue could trump that. The zeal of new believers like Tim continually challenges me. Am I keener to make broad points about values and faith or will I actually get to the root of the problem in conversation with people? Will I actually ask them who they think Jesus is? And subtly different, who will they say that he is?

I fear the devil has cleverly distracted us from playing with our strongest suit. These days, if we're brave, we may talk about God or religion in public debate or general conversation, but we really struggle to say the word 'Jesus'. Jesus' name has a power that it seems we, the devil and the world are scared of. Gemma's reaction is a good example. To speak of Jesus rather than just 'faith' has become a cultural taboo. He's just too 'in your face'. It's just too personal. Keep it vague and fluffy. As the feted journalist Polly Toynbee said, 'The only faith that is wanted in the public square is a moribund faith.'

There is a generation of young people like Tim, Lewis and Shaun who are prepared, in whatever situation, to have the name Jesus on their lips. What a challenge they present to us. In our adult sophistication we have managed to brush him under the carpet. We will speak about him to those 'in the know', and we will sing his name repeatedly with great fervour, but we don't seem able to introduce into everyday conversation the man who we claim to be the most important factor in our lives.

It's because we have all become expert people-pleasers, and as we introduce the name of Jesus into conversation, we can feel people's discomfort. Something spiritual is happening. There is a battleground here. Satan knows that if Jesus is part of conversation, there is not much he can do to prevent people encountering the perfect man who was God. When you get talking about him, no one has a bad word to say about him, the historical evidence backs up his existence (no matter what Dan Brown's wife grabbed off the internet), and it doesn't take a degree in New Testament theology to be able to debunk the 'Jesus was just a good man' line of reasoning. Satan knows that if he lets Jesus into normal conversation, he's sunk, so rather than fight a battle and lose, he cleverly fools everyone into shying away from it.

Simon Peter was not one to shrink from the battle, even if it did not look exactly as he had imagined it. The other disciples deflected the question sideways:

> They replied, 'Some say John the Baptist; others say Elijah; and still others, Jeremiah or one of the prophets.'

They were happy to talk about what someone else thought, but they weren't volunteering what they thought. As ever, they left that up to Peter. He was the one who stepped up to the plate. Likewise, Tim was the one person in that carriage who got up to see if things were all right up at the front of the train. Peter was willing to make another mistake. And if he got this question wrong, it would be a big mistake. If he got this question wrong it would mean that the months he had spent journeying with Jesus would have been utterly pointless. It's not like there wasn't a lot riding on this question. It's the equivalent of Chris Tarrant staring at you as you ponder the million-pound question, with no audience to ask, and no friends to phone. You can almost hear the tension-building music in the background. 'Who do *you* say that I am?'

It's easy to discuss someone else's faith or someone else's struggles and opinions. It's easy to deflect. Imagine the Son of God intensely, but lovingly, staring you in the face right now, saying these words: 'But what about *you*? Who do *you* say I am?' (italics mine). 'I don't care who your vicar, or your Sunday school teacher, or your mum, or your dad, or your best friend, or your dentist say I am. Who do you say I am?'

We have found that this has been a phenomenally releasing way to encourage young people into connecting with God. We often ask this question by means of animations, readings or video clips, then we provide various media for young people to express their answers. Some will just speak it out. Some will write it on sheets of paper. Some will use art and craft. Others will create computer-screen displays. The fantastic thing is that their own expression is *their* answer. They own it, and they do not feel that anyone has manipulated them into making that expression. We provide the space and allow people to honestly articulate their answer to that question.

We work with many unchurched young people, so their honest answers, which we encourage, can be along the lines of 'I haven't a clue who you are', or 'You're the bloke who took away my Mum', or 'I wish I knew who you are, but I don't really know yet'. These moments are often the start of a journey of faith. These honest answers give YFC youth-workers a context for working with these young people.

How will we ever know where young people are at if we always tell them what to sing? If all we do is make the music groovy, but then tell them to sing a certain set of words, because 'that's what you should be thinking', how is that the start of an honest relationship with God? I'll tell you what that's called. It's called religion.

In the worship experiences that we craft, we must leave space for asking questions and honest expression, otherwise church will never be a place of real connection with God for young people. They will speak the code while in church, but then find more harmful ways of expressing their anger, frustration, passions or rejection while they're outside.

Jesus was the king of asking questions, yet we have become princes of the dogmatic statement. And as we look at the media's portrayal of youth culture, often our statements become more and more desperate, leading less and less people to respond. Come to think of it, maybe that's why people aren't responding so much. How do you respond when you haven't been asked anything?

Verbalizing

Another reason why Jesus asked the disciples the big question was that he knew that it was vital for their discipleship journey that they should be able to publicly state who they believed him to be. As Paul would write in Romans:

> ... if you confess with your mouth, 'Jesus is Lord,' and believe in your heart that God raised him from the dead, you will be saved. For it is with your heart that you believe and are justified, and it is with your mouth that you confess and are saved.   (Romans 10:9–10)

This dynamic is why so many young people who experience a gap-year programme with Youth For Christ find that their lives are radically changed. They have been through a year where, week by week, they have been provided with opportunities in various contexts to publicly state who they believe Jesus to be. These contexts may be anything from after-school clubs, concerts and assemblies, to young offenders' institutions, PHSE classes and youth centres. Their faith is refined in the fire of interacting with other young people, who will have different answers to that vital question, or may have never actually thought about it.

However, you can imagine how demanding this can be, which is why young people are placed in small teams that can pray for and support one another. They are also tooled up by a rolling programme of training throughout the year from experts in the field and those who have gone before them. Year after year, reading the feedback of the young people who have been through the programmes convinces me that the key moments of growth for those involved have been those times when they have been stretched beyond their comfort zones and have 'confessed him with their lips'.

Jemima's story is typical of someone who returned to her old context and had an impact on her peers far beyond anything she would have had if she had stayed in the comfort of a 'normal life'. While I ran YFC's band, TVB, we often visited some of the band members' home towns, playing concerts in their old schools. I loved to watch teachers' faces when the 'home-town' band member would share something of their story in front of concert or assembly audiences, which can be pretty intimidating crowds! The teachers would struggle to believe that the shy, shuffling pupil, lacking in self-confidence, whom they once knew, had become someone who was not only holding everyone's attention, but holding them in the palm of their hand.

Of course, there are physical factors at play – some practice, some confidence, the strength of a team standing behind you, but something has also shifted in the spiritual realm. There has been a step-up in their devotional lives and a regular infilling of the Spirit – both part of the discipline of team life. Later we'll look at the similar transformation that occurred in Peter. His first 'assembly' had thousands of listeners, and you couldn't say that he had a small impact!

Return to sender

Having listened to many young people tell me their stories in researching this book, I cannot help but smile when I read Luke chapter 10. Luke is obviously experiencing similar levels of excitement as mine. Having recorded Jesus' departing instructions in verse 16, he publishes their gap-year report in the very next verse:

The seventy-two returned with joy and said, 'Lord, even the demons submit to us in your name.'   (Luke 10:17)

I think we can safely say it has gone well! The joy that they are returning with is the same joy that I have heard over and over again from young people relaying their stories after they have truly stepped out into adventures with God. I wish you could have heard Tim's compassion as he spoke about Pabon, and his delirious excitement on reporting that he had come to faith. I wish you could see the look on the faces of any of our bands when they return from their first ever week working in schools. Much as we try to inspire them with the hope that they will have a real impact, they don't really believe it until they see it happening before their very eyes. You can see the difference it has made to their bodies, never mind their hearts, minds and spirits. The hunched-over teenager look has gone and they look taller! They realize that the gospel really does work and that young people still crave good news. The problem is that most of the time, nobody has the nerve to tell them that there is some. The other realization is that God can use *them*! They're still aware of all their hang-ups and issues that they thought would need to be completely sorted before they were of any use to the kingdom, but he still used them! Not only that, but he used them through the gifts he had given them in music, listening, praying, sport, administration, drama or dance. When that happens, they feel alive in a way that they've never felt before, doing perhaps what they were born to do.

By the way, for the record, in the midst of my excitement here, I am not exaggerating. I know that feeling. There is nothing like it in the world. You hear the stories of the lives that Jesus has changed forever and the heart-breaking stories of those who have been hampered by their backgrounds or by sins they can't get away from. You hear the stories of teachers who have had to re-examine their own attitudes to Christianity. You read the letters from head-teachers who have been blown away by the positive impact that a team have had on a school's atmosphere. In short, you realize that God is bigger and busier than you or I could ever imagine.

Before a fall

Jesus stepped into all the excitement with a reminder of where the power they had just experienced had come from and a warning not to let pride get the better of them:

> I have given you authority to trample on snakes and scorpions and to overcome all the power of the enemy; nothing will harm you. However, do not rejoice that the spirits submit to you, but rejoice that your names are written in heaven. (Luke 10:19–20)

Unfortunately, I know how important Jesus' words of warning are. The classic scenario is this: (1) We pray like crazy for God to move in a certain event or situation. (2) He does. (3) In our excitement, we text everybody under the sun to tell them, but forget to thank God and give him the glory for it. (4) We start believing subconsciously that it is our skills or abilities that are doing the business. I know how important the warning is because I have been there and done that and bought too many T-shirts to mention.

Peter gets tripped up by his pride on a few occasions in the gospels. You don't have to read very far between the lines to guess who the chief protagonist was during all those 'Who is the greatest disciple?' discussions that kept cropping up. Peter and John obviously had a strong relationship, but I am sure Peter struggled with 'the disciple whom Jesus loved'. We would all want to be Jesus' favourite. In John 21 Peter is enjoying some quality time with Jesus, but gets a bit of a surprise when Jesus lets him in on how he's going to die (verses 18–19). Perhaps Peter hears the sound of eager shuffling feet, and he furtively looks back over his shoulder to see John following them. Not that Peter is competitive at all (of course not!), but his immediate question is, 'What about him?' (verse 21). I can imagine the angle of Peter's neck as he inclines it towards Jesus and utters that question with the whisper of one craving public intimacy. However, Jesus sees straight to his heart and calmly rebukes him (again!):

> Jesus answered, 'If I want him to remain alive until I return, what is that to you? You must follow me.' (verse 22)

This is the final act of the Peter–John sideshow that, I suspect, was at the heart of the argument in Luke 22:24:

> Also a dispute arose among them as to which of them was considered to be greatest.

Ironically, this occurs in the Upper Room immediately after they have shared the first ever communion together. Over years of church history, this has been a meal that has brought reconciliation and repentance between warring individuals and church factions, in the manner of Jesus' instruction in Matthew 5:23–24:

> Therefore, if you are offering your gift at the altar and there remember that your brother has something against you, leave your gift there in front of the altar. First go and be reconciled to your brother; then come and offer your gift.

It is almost perversely encouraging that the first disciples were able to make such a hash of it, letting their goldfish-sized memory get the better of them. So after this most holy of moments, how could such a dispute have arisen? The key lies in the fact that it was a meal. The disciples were reclining around the table.

In their culture, where you sat around the table was of optimum importance in revealing your status amongst those present. The seats on either side of the host were the most coveted, and the further away you got, the less important you would look. On this most significant of nights, did the disciples care where they were sitting? You bet they did. And did a certain Simon Peter care which position he was in? Of course not, as he would obviously be sitting at Jesus' right hand as his main man. Except he wasn't. Whether he was gazumped or whether it was just a freak result of a first-century game of musical chairs (without the chairs), we will never know, but John's Gospel makes it clear that John was reclining next to Jesus, and that Peter had to motion to him to ask Jesus the crucial question about who the betrayer was. Judas was probably on the other side of Jesus, as Luke 22:21 suggests:

But the hand of him who is going to betray me is with mine on the table.

This thought is strengthened by the disciples' confusion about why Judas suddenly leaves the room:

Since Judas had charge of the money, some thought Jesus was telling him to buy what was needed for the Feast, or to give something to the poor.
(John 13:29)

If Judas was close by, it would explain why not everyone heard or fully understood when Jesus said to him, 'What you are about to do, do quickly' (John 13:27). So this was more of an aside or a whisper, rather than a grand statement.

All of which leads me to believe that Peter wasn't a happy camper! It doesn't take much deduction to guess who would have the reason and the nerve/foot-in-mouth capability to bring up the subject straight after the last supper. Perhaps he suggested another game of musical non-chairs, but whatever happened, their pride got the better of them and they were suddenly behaving like the world and not like the bringers of the upside-down kingdom that was being promised.

As so often happened, Jesus stepped in to sort it out. He'd already gone out of his way just a few hours before to demonstrate true leadership with the whole foot-washing thing, but it obviously needed saying one more time:

> Jesus said to them, 'The kings of the Gentiles lord it over them; and those who exercise authority over them call themselves Benefactors. But you are not to be like that. Instead, the greatest among you should be like the youngest, and the one who rules like the one who serves. For who is greater, the one who is at the table or the one who serves? Is it not the one who is at the table? But I am among you as one who serves.
>
> (Luke 22:25–27)

It's a sobering tale for all of us, especially people involved in what gets called 'full-time ministry'. You can see how in the story of Lewis, his pride tripped him up. He rested back on the fact that God had called him, and took his foot off the pedal of his relationship with Jesus. He made an utterly false connection that because he had seen God use him, he would be impervious to the attacks of the devil, and that they would have no long-term impact. This is always a danger for YFC staff and volunteers, especially when they are seeing God do amazing things in their vicinity. The job of mentoring and giving pastoral support to these young evangelists is vital. They are encouraged into accountable relationships, where brutal honesty is fostered. These young people are on the front line, and we have to acknowledge the intense stimulation they undergo from all the media and the crazy world that surrounds them, especially in the area of sex and sexuality. Realistically, it can be a matter of when the stumble will come, rather than if. Jesus' grace-laden restoration of Peter on the beach in John 21 is of vital importance. We'll get there soon.

And a little child...

We were back in Luke 10 before our important diversion, with Jesus making sure the disciples don't get carried away on their triumphant return. But this doesn't take away from the fact that he's loving it!

> At that time Jesus, full of joy through the Holy Spirit, said, 'I praise you, Father, Lord of heaven and earth, because you have hidden these things from the wise and learned, and revealed them to little children. Yes, Father, for this was your good pleasure. (Luke 10:21)

I can testify to the fact that there is nothing more satisfying than seeing young people who you have mentored 'do the business'. I guess the feeling must be akin to seeing your young child walk for the first time. Their joy brings you joy. This section of the passage also underlines the upside-down values of God's kingdom that is being announced through Jesus and his followers. Could it really be that these things are being hidden from the wise and learned? Could it really be that the secrets of life are being revealed to and, furthermore, spread by these working men? When Jesus associates the disciples with little children here, we have to see that he is not belittling them, but paying them a compliment. He doesn't look at the world with the same eyes that we do. He is not fooled by power and wealth. He sees to the heart. He longs for people to come to him with the openness and innocence of children:

> And he said: 'I tell you the truth, unless you change and become like little children, you will never enter the kingdom of heaven.' (Matthew 18:3)

So in our day, is it possible that Jesus still reveals his plans and leads his people through 'the little children'? There are echoes here of Isaiah 11:6:

The wolf will live with the lamb,
the leopard will lie down with the goat,
the calf and the lion and the yearling together;
and a little child will lead them.

I have seen much first-hand evidence that this is what is taking place inside and outside churches all over the UK. This has especially been through programmes of word-and-deed evangelism like 'Soul in the City' (London), 'Message 2000' (Manchester), 'Merseyfest' (Merseyside), 'Streetreach' (Belfast), 'NE1' (the North-East), and countless others in other towns. The energy that young people have brought to these programmes has been phenomenal. Their desire to roll up their sleeves and serve has been breathtaking. There are hundreds of stories of communities that have been impacted. Even more significantly, perhaps, there are many testimonies of young people who have caught the bug of evangelism and have gone home to their own context to inspire similar efforts. This energy is being harnessed and carried to the rest of the church by Hope2008 (www.hope08.com). Spearheaded by Roy Crowne (YFC), Andy Hawthorne (Message) and Mike Pilavachi (Soul Survivor), it is a call to churches up and down the country to step up what they are doing in evangelism. Some examples of specific goals are for the whole church to dispense one million hours of kindness, to get 100,000 people into evangelistic prayer triplets, and to facilitate thousands of opportunities for faith-sharing like concerts, barbeques and assemblies. To quote the Hope2008 website, the 'hope' is that it will facilitate a year of intensified, united, focused prayer and activities, communicating the Gospel through words and actions, and creating a lasting legacy of both physical and spiritual change in the lives of communities and individuals.

The children have led. Let us follow.

Head-hunting

Jesus continues on this theme:

> For I tell you that many prophets and kings wanted to see what you see but did not see it, and to hear what you hear but did not hear it.   (Luke 10:24)

He wants to let the disciples know what a privileged position they hold, but is also desperate to underline the fact that earthly high rank counts for nothing in his coming kingdom. We, however, live in a world where status and celebrity count for everything. How do we square these opposite realities? Whether on the school playground, or in any gathering of movers and shakers, people gravitate towards those with most perceived power. How much time do we waste trying to curry favour with those who possess earthly power? This is simply not the Jesus way. That is never more in evidence than in Jesus' selection of Peter as the 'rock' on which he will build his church:

> And I tell you that you are Peter, and on this rock I will build my church, and the gates of Hades will not overcome it.   (Matthew 16:18)

Let's suppose for a moment that Jesus has employed you as a head-hunter to prowl around the Middle East of the first century AD and find the right man for the job. He will be the foundation of Jesus' church. The employee will not own the church, or even build it. Jesus makes it clear that *he* will be doing the building.

So since Jesus has already come up with the business plan and the branding, are you looking not so much for an ideas man, but more for a good manager and facilitator? Are you looking for a good salesman who can get people on side? Someone who can convince a sceptical public that this really is what they desperately need? Are you looking for a hard-nosed Alan Sugar type, a dreaming Richard Branson, an ear-pleasing Tony Blair, or an inspiring Anita Roddick?

There must be a progressive, young religious leader, open to new ideas, but respected by the establishment. Surely someone who is based in the capital would be best placed to set up the networks and structures necessary. Someone with a bit of money behind them wouldn't be a bad idea either. There'll need to be a lot of advertising and marketing shekels spent. If they could be good-looking and articulate, that would probably help as well.

Something tells me that Peter the fisherman is not even making it onto your short-list. Yet it is Peter the unschooled fisherman whom Jesus chooses to be the foundation of the movement that will change history forever. There is no area of life – cultural, philosophical, physical, intellectual, political, sexual, spiritual (hopefully!) – that the church has not had an impact on. It has gone from the modesty of a Galilean jetty to the furthest corners of the earth in a very short space of time. God's plans are so much bigger than we could ever imagine. Jesus showed what kind of movement he was beginning by making it abundantly clear what kind of man should be its leader. He wasn't looking at what you or I look at:

> But God chose the foolish things of the world to shame the wise; God chose the weak things of the world to shame the strong.   (1 Corinthians 1:27)

It is to these foolish nobodies that God has always revealed his plans and his heart. I truly believe that often these nobodies are very young. I know two towns where it has been the teenage volunteers of a YFC centre who managed to get all the churches together where many adults had failed before them.

So let's adjust our radar. So often our attention is only grabbed by the blips of powerful people, especially those who are 'names' in the church. Let's be ready and willing to follow 'the least of these', as in doing so you may be following any number of now-and-future leaders.

There was a jaw-dropping quote in the BBC's recent drama series *The Amazing Mrs Pritchard*, about a normal housewife who becomes prime minister:

> Every so often someone comes along and changes things forever, and it's never the person anyone expected it to be.

8 Car Wash

Amy

Pushing her trolley up the cereal aisle, Amy thinks to herself, 'I need one that my brother will eat.' She surveys the coloured boxes. Not Coco Pops – not healthy enough for Mum. Not Bran Flakes – too boring for him. How to choose?

She suddenly realizes that this decision is simple compared to the one she has to make about her future. As her focus on the boxes begins to blur in front of her, she concludes, 'No wonder I can't decide about my life. I can't even choose which stupid box of cereal to buy! How has this happened to me?' Leaving Tony the Tiger behind, her procrastinating feet wander off to other aisles as her mind wanders back to where it all began...

Amy didn't know how she had ended up there. She hadn't wanted to go. She was quite happy at home, working at the pub and the hair-dresser's, surrounded by her drinking buddies and her older boyfriend. But her mum had said to her that she really needed Amy there – she wanted her help looking after a girl with cerebral palsy. Amy had thought it through and eventually concluded that, however boring, a week off from work couldn't be a bad thing. Surely she could suppress her inde-pendent, feisty character for seven days. It didn't need to be expressed to such an extent anyway, when she was out of range of all her brothers and sisters. At the event, it turned out that all she was expected to do was to take the girl to the morning and evening meetings. She had always enjoyed taking care of people with special needs, and the after-noons would be hers to do with as she pleased.

As soon as she arrived Amy knew that her apprehension was justi-fied. The place may have looked (and smelt) like Butlins, but it was cer-tainly unlike any holiday she had been on before. Huge marquees had been erected all over the site, and smiley Jesus freaks, laden with Bibles and notebooks, were coming and going from them constantly. Strange music would stream from the tents, stopping Amy in her tracks. Everyone was singing together. Everyone seemed to like each other. This was a totally alien environment. Normally Amy would mind her own business on holiday and only engage with her family, but this week peo-ple kept striking up friendly conversation and showing an interest in her life. She couldn't understand it.

Sitting in the wheelchair section at the front of meetings made the conference speakers hard to ignore. Amy had tried hard to fill her mind with other things, and avoid the preacher's gaze, but it was impossible. By the end of the week she was listening to every word, and although she didn't quite understand what was going on, she knew something inside her had changed. The atmosphere was so unlike anything Amy had experienced before. It induced the desire to shed a few tears and a sudden need to question her life. As she sat cross-legged outside the main marquee, soaking up the songs drifting through the tent flaps, she could hardly believe how much had changed within her in only a week. It was the last day and she didn't want to move. She wasn't content any more to be selfish, to be ordinary, to be like everyone else she knew back home. She closed her eyes, humming along to the tune, and found herself praying that her life would change – forever.

Returning home at the end of the week, reality looked and sounded very different through Amy's senses. She found herself, for the first time in years, in church not just once, but twice in a month. Her most significant discovery was that people were smiling at her in the street. That had never happened before. It took her a while to work out that it was because she was smiling. The daily conversation in the salon left her, at the end of each day, wanting more. All of a sudden life felt like it was being turned inside out, upside down and back to front.

Amy had always skipped school. She had missed half her exams and had then dropped out of college within months of registering. Messing around with her mates had been far more appealing. But now she was different. Out of nowhere had come a drive to be an auxiliary nurse. Amy found herself eagerly scanning hospital websites. She downloaded some forms about a job nearby, and filled out the application. She didn't even know what a bed-pan was but somehow she knew she had to go for it. Her new-found enthusiasm got her the job.

Smoking no longer had the same appeal. She had always felt more at ease with a cigarette in her hand. They made her feel like an adult – capable and confident, even though a frightened, confused teenager hid behind the façade. After six years, Amy quit on the spot, with no after-effects or cravings. Her friends found this difficult to understand, but no amount of persuading could change her mind. She had always done so many things to fit in. Now she felt able to stand up for herself and make her own decisions. A need to be part of the crowd was being replaced with a new desire to go against the flow.

Taking her driving test, gaining nursing qualifications, and splitting up with her boyfriend – all choices that Amy made in quick succession. Ending her relationship was an especially agonizing decision. She had known for a while that she wouldn't spend the rest of her life with this guy, but something had always prevented her from letting go. It was now becoming clear that the physical intimacy of sex had created a bond between them that she was struggling to break. A part of her had always felt that the physical relationship between them was wrong – it may even have been the reason why she had found herself drawing the line at moving in with him. When she dreamt about her future, he didn't feature in it. It was the toughest decision yet, but Amy made it.

As she put down the sweaty hand-set to end the abrupt conversation with her boyfriend, she panicked. What was she doing? She had already stripped her life of so much familiarity – now even her boyfriend, whom she loved, was about to become only a memory. Church suddenly seemed harder to engage with. Her friends were encouraging her to party hard. Although Amy knew that they only wanted to help her get over her break-up, and indulged them for a few months, she couldn't help noticing how empty it all felt.

Easter was coming round again. The staff at Butlins would soon be welcoming the Christians through their gates. Memories of last year, her experience of God, and the commitments she'd made, all came flooding back to her, and all she wanted to do was go again. She begged her mum and dad, and they agreed. Amy marked off the days on her calendar, praying for the week of camp to come quickly.

Eventually she was there, arriving at the entrance for the second time, filled with expectation and excitement. She promised herself that she would attend every single meeting – not because she felt she should, but because she wanted to. She even went to some of them on her own, because she was so eager to focus on God.

It was as if someone turned a light on inside Amy that week. People remarked on the joy that they saw in her face. She felt that she was being opened up and filled with something special. One evening someone explained the story of Pentecost from the Bible, and Amy knew that this new experience was God coming to live in her by his Holy Spirit. All week the people had been talking about Jesus, the Son of God, and now she wanted to commit her life to serve him. The encounter was real. After one of the sessions, Amy's mind was overcome with questions: 'What am I going to do now? Where am I going?' As she walked back to her chalet, one of the exhibition stalls caught her eye. Pinned to it was a piece of paper on which were written the words:

'For I know the plans I have for you,' declares the Lord, 'plans to prosper you and not to harm you, plans to give you hope and a future.' (Jeremiah 29:11)

Amy couldn't believe her eyes when she read the same words on her cake at her baptism a few months later. She had gone from being a scared young girl, desperate to fit in at school, doing what she thought would make her happy, to being a confident woman, standing up for things that mattered and unafraid of being different. Her whole outlook on life was transformed. This Easter had created an even greater change in her life than the previous one. This time she wanted to throw herself into the life of the church, work with teenagers and publicly declare her faith. Amy didn't want life to revolve around her own plans and decisions; she needed to know God's plans for her life. She wanted to put Christ first in everything.

It frustrated her when she shared her new-found belief with her mates in the pub – they were more interested in the fact that she had decided not to sleep with anyone before getting married, than the fact that Jesus had died for them. Having invited loads of her friends to her baptism, Amy was deeply upset when three of her closest mates texted her to say they were bailing out just an hour before it took place. Amy put it down to their fear of the unknown. She just desperately wanted them to discover the truth that she had found and she knew it could change their lives as much as it had hers. However, Amy was thankful to God when some lads she'd been mates with at school showed up to witness her getting dunked.

Amy loved auxiliary nursing and hoped to work her way onto a full-time nursing degree course. But a tension emerged: the shifts she worked prevented her from throwing herself into all that was going on at church. Amazingly, as she prayed for an opportunity to spend more time with young people in the church, a new day job in the Day Case Unit became available. It was fewer hours and less money, but she didn't care because it would release her to do more with the young people. Although the interview process challenged her patience, she got the job and found herself able to increase her time and develop new ways to work with the younger people in the church.

However, the tension wasn't removed. Amy really thought that God had been leading her into full-time nursing. Everything had pointed to that – everyone loved her at work, she was making progress in each area, and changing to the Day Case Unit had occurred at just the right time. But as she immersed herself in organizing a youth event, in teaching eleven- to fourteen-year-olds on a Sunday morning, in serving them on the summer camps, she discovered an increasing passion and a new set of skills for working with teenagers. This was something she could also do, and do well.

The more involved Amy became, the more she wanted to do. As she prayed about the nursing and the youth work, seeking advice from various people, she longed for clarity on which path she should take. Pursuing the nursing option would mean moving hundreds of miles away to do the degree. Everyone had an opinion on Amy's future, and yet she wasn't convinced which (if any) were the definitive words from God. And she couldn't shake the nagging reality that the church needed a youth worker. She had a strange pull to speak to kids on street corners; the idea of a drop-in centre occurred to her; and the fact that there was nothing for the fifteen-plus age group in the church kept bugging her. Combining her two passions was another option – getting involved with young people in her future university town – but leaving behind the teenagers she now loved would be hard. Amy realized that encountering

Christ and letting him take priority in her life was challenging. It demanded sacrifices that she wasn't sure she could make.

As she returns to the cereal section with a full trolley, she drifts back to the here and now. 'What am I doing? I need to make a decision!' Finally she makes her breakfast selection: oats. That was simpler than deciding on a cereal to suit everyone. Let them eat porridge. Amy heads to the till with a packed trolley, wishing there was a third way that might solve the dilemma about her young people and nursing.

But as the automatic doors of the supermarket slide open, a cool breeze catches her cheeks and snaps her away from her present indecision to the big picture of her life. From nowhere, some words that a friend had read to her recently flash through her mind: 'Whether you turn to the right or to the left, your ears will hear a voice behind you, saying, "This is the way; walk in it."'

This reassurance was multiplied by the voice in her head reminding her that two years ago, the only decisions she was making were 'wax or gel?' by day, and 'pineapple or cranberry Breezer?' by night.

Life really had changed!

9 Pile-up

Brian

Brian Summers couldn't sleep. His head was on its spin cycle, imagining a nightmare scenario:

The competitors for the Olympic 100 metres final are lined up like sticks of human dynamite. But the runner in lane 3 is crouched a good twenty metres behind his adversaries. It will take him a few seconds to even make it as far as the blocks. No one seems to notice this obvious anomaly. The fuses are lit. It's an explosive start. He makes up ground, but no matter how hard he tries, he simply isn't getting close to the others...

Brian had felt like this all of his life. No matter how much effort he put in, there seemed to be a constant gap between his experience and that of the other kids his age. For some reason, things came more naturally to them. They didn't seem to struggle with the same sort of stuff he struggled with. People told him it was because he'd never known his dad, or because his mum was a witch (in the literal sense), but he didn't really understand why that should make a difference. As he always said, 'You don't miss what you've never had.'

The God thing had changed everything, but right at this moment, those twenty metres seemed like a mile. He was staying at his youth worker Tim's house for a few days, because yet another foster family had reported, 'It's just not working out.' Things always followed the same pattern. Each new family started out with a lot of promise, but after a while he couldn't maintain the energy to keep impressing them. Eventually the ground rules with regard to curfews or tidiness would take their toll on his patience. He just wasn't used to living like that. He never had been. He had really prayed about it this time, pleading with God that this arrangement would work out. He really was doing his best. With the help of Tim, he was learning some social skills, but when a swear-word slipped out, he just couldn't cope with the looks that he received. It sent him back into his vicious cycle of feeling bad about himself, and leaning towards behaviour that confirmed his suspicions.

Everyone kept going the extra mile for Brian, as there actually was so much about him that inspired those who met him. He had an ability to relate to anyone with that cheeky half-smile that made you feel understood. If there was physical work to be done, he would be the first in line to help. There was a vat of affection for him at church because they knew how far he had come in such a short space of time. They knew how hard it was for any of the young people from the Oakwood Estate to escape its vices. Positive role models there were as common as mean-ingful debate in *Heat* magazine.

He surveyed the room in which he was failing to nod off. It was hard to look at a new room without the old memories flooding back. Each new room used to represent a new opportunity. Another set of drawers or shelves to rifle through, another secret stash to find. Old habits die hard, and within a few seconds he knew exactly what would disappear first, and where his escape route could be. But that couldn't happen now – could it? Things were different – weren't they? Laptop. Minidisc player. DVD carry-case. Targets acquired.

Brian had been the ring-leader of a crew of mischief-making lads from his estate. He was short but well built, with a spiky haircut that gave him that 'dangerous enough to be interesting' look. The scars on his hands and face did nothing to arrest that image. Throughout his early teenage years he had developed a talent for getting into cars, partly because it was a challenge, but mostly because they were parked there right in front of him while he had nothing else to do. It seemed like an easy way of gaining respect. But the people whose respect and attention he gained encouraged him to try cannabis and then crack cocaine, put-ting him in a position whereby stealing was no longer an optional hobby, but an essential way to fund an addiction. But right in the midst of all this, a pretty girl had convinced him to come to the local parish church youth group. There he found a new sense of community, where he didn't always feel the need to impress. At a summer camp he unmistakably encountered the reality of Jesus and started communicating with him, which had led to twelve months of being clean and being a very different person.

He could hardly believe that he had even let his brain wander into the territory of stealing from Tim. He'd got away with things before (he could be pretty persuasive when it was called for), but how could he even think about nicking stuff from here? What a risk! The reality was that the thrill of this risk actually poured petrol on the insubstantial flame of an idea.

Surely he couldn't? Could he? It would be like a kick in the guts to Tim. Of course, he could never tell Tim this, but he pretty much owed him everything. All the progress he'd made in the last few months could be traced back to moments where Tim had intervened, even though Brian could never understand why he bothered. Whether it was those long nights sitting in the Casualty waiting room, the spoken words that acted like an alarm clock to his soul, or the text messages that just made him feel wanted, Brian knew that his journey would have looked very different without Tim's influence. In fact, apart from Tim, Brian didn't really have any other fixed points in his life. No one else was always there, always available, and always in possession of the right word at the right time. He was certain that this must have had a negative impact on Tim's own social life, but he never seemed to complain. Plenty of other people seemed to have words they wanted him to hear, but what they said usually got lost in translation. Brian reckoned that you only listen to people when you know that they listen to you.

All these thoughts were percolating around Brian's head as he pulled his 'B' clothes on. His limited funds meant that he needed a system. Systems were good. Systems were what had enabled him to stay sharp and ahead of the other losers on the estate. When you had chemicals in your body, you needed reliable systems, because sometimes you couldn't trust yourself to think rationally. His systems included where he stashed money, how and when he answered his mobile, and which routes he would take through town.

This particular system was less private, but no less important. His 'B' clothes walked an important tightrope. It was suspended between garnering enough respect from 'the lads', but not so much that he was obviously trying to win the approval of the ladies. It was the 'I don't have to try, and I'm not trying (honestly)' look. It had been a while since he'd worn these clothes, and he wasn't even sure why he'd instinctively grabbed for them. Recently he'd mostly been in 'A' mode (because the girls at church were really good looking), or 'C' mode (because most other times, he was starting to care less and less about what other people thought of him, and more and more about what God thought of him). But at this moment something strange was going on inside him, and rather than explore what it was and face up to it, it felt easier to paper over the cracks, sorting out the exterior things he could control.

Still feeling guilty that he'd even let the earlier thoughts into his head, that night he sought the comfort of familiar surroundings and old 'friends'. He felt simultaneously reassured and uneasy. The backdrop of urine-dowsed lifts and designer concrete fuelled a strange kind of superiority complex in his head, but no mental state was lasting for long tonight. His old crew were surprised to see him and at first didn't know how to react. Everyone looked at everyone else, hoping to glean the appropriate tone and attitude towards Brian. Obviously no one had stepped up into leadership in his absence.

'Who do you think you are?' cried a voice in his head. 'You'll never be the head honcho of this patch again. Wise up! They know about the God stuff. Your stock price has gone through the floor.'

His anger flared up. 'I'll show you!' he thought to himself, striding towards the dealer who was hovering a hospitable distance from the group.

Twenty minutes later he was the life and soul of the party again. The prodigal son had come home. The other lads' guilt had been swept away when they realized that it wasn't possible to change after all. There is always something good about making people feel good about themselves. This was fast becoming the party of the year. One thing led to another, and soon all of Brian's old bravado was back. This was something he could touch, something he could feel, something that flicked all the switches of rebellion, experience and danger that connected in his head to cause one massive short-circuit. The sparks that were flying were actually part of the attraction. The next twenty-four hours were a bit of a blur, but at the end of them one fact was crystal clear. He had no money left.

For his next hit, there was a desperate need for more cash, and to chicken out now would jeopardize the street cred he had been so lucky to salvage. All his inhibitions from the previous day had been dumped in a duffel bag and tossed over the fence of his life's playground. He realized that by a happy coincidence, there was a youth event going on at the church that Friday night, meaning that there definitely wouldn't be anyone at Tim's house. His recent stay meant that he had already sussed the best way in, where no one would be able to see his expertise at work. He didn't ever stop to reflect on how automatic this was feeling.

A mere forty-eight hours earlier, he had been praying for someone else from the youth group. His friend Phil had been struggling to cope with his parents' separation, and Brian knew that what he had prayed for him had made a real impact. It's not that that didn't seem real now, it was just a different kind of real – an alternative reality.

It wasn't hard to recruit a couple of willing accomplices for the task. He had presented the job as practically a fait accompli, with his old consummate confidence. The sad thing was that the two younger lads now succumbing to Brian's negative influence had also been on the receiving end of positive peer pressure. They had been along to church with him because, if it was good enough for Brian, it was good enough for them. This was partly why Tim had invested so much time and love in Brian. He could see that he was the key link in a potential kingdom chain that could connect further into the estate than the church had ever been before.

It was 8:05 p.m. – early enough to leave time to make an alibi appearance at the youth event later, but late enough to avoid the scenario in which anyone needed to nip back to the house for that DVD or guitar that they had forgotten. They approached the house through the dark cover of the adjoining park.

With his sentries posted in the dusk, Brian found a concrete block suitable for the task. It had to be heavy enough to smash through the double glazing, but not so heavy that he couldn't hurl it with great force towards the window. Tim and his housemates would later find that block resting at the foot of their now-dented fridge-freezer which stood a whole three metres from the window! A post-burglary urine sample would have shown up an awful lot of adrenaline, as well as the illegal substances.

Once inside, the first job was to find an appropriately sized bag so that the exit from the premises could look natural if necessary. Swagger does contain the word 'swag', after all. This wasn't hard to come by, and the trusting youth workers didn't even have locks on their doors, so the supermarket sweep didn't take very long at all. However, there was one moment when Brian stumbled. As he leant down to tug the laptop power cable out of the wall socket, his nose rested for a moment on Tim's bed-side table, right beside the Bible that Brian had been reading while sitting on that bed just a few days before. For a split second he froze, as if reminded of another world. But he was committed now. There was no turning back.

By 8.35 p.m., Tim was minus one laptop, one minidisc player, and many DVDs. Brian was £150 better off, having reacquainted himself with another old friend, who was more than happy to 'help him out' by taking the rapidly cooling goods off his hands.

By 8.45, Brian had sneaked in at the back of the youth event. People were used to him being late. No one thought it unusual. They were just glad that he was there at all. Tim especially was relieved, and even though he was leading worship at the time, he threw a wink in Brian's direction. Brian returned it with interest like a top-spin forehand. He hit it with some degree of confidence. At least he didn't blow him a kiss.

By 8.55, Brian was holding in a knowing smile as the collection plate came round and by 9.30, he was leaving without much fuss to get back to his new/old friends.

Cue another party on the estate. Cue a strangely renewed sense of identity. Cue the Sunday-morning denials at church that have a familiar ring to them.

Cue a sense of hundreds of hours of investment wasted.

Cut.

10 Back-seat Driving

Evan

What begins as a tiny little seed in your mind can grow into a giant tree, whose branches reach into every area of your life. It can be planted by a misunderstanding, or a difference in opinion, or an alternative way of handling things. Then continued exposure to the same problems or frustrations, unhelpful discussions with folk who feel the same way, or even discovering that your disappointment is well founded, provide the fertile soil. If cynicism is allowed to hustle its way into your life like this, it is extremely difficult to unearth it.

It took a long time for Evan to realize that he had allowed a seed of cynicism to be planted in his life. This fourteen-year-old was a leader, not a follower, immensely confident that his opinion on most issues was

the right one. His competitive streak stretched equally into church buildings and sports halls.

He didn't think he was the one with the issues. 'They' were the folks
who had welcomed this funny 'revival' – allowing strange new experiences of God to infiltrate his church. He had been wary from the start.
Should people really be roaring like lions, clucking like cockerels, shaking all over and falling dramatically to the floor? It all seemed to be
about people having an 'outward experience' of God. They would stand
there as consumers, waiting to be prayed for, so that they could receive
some instant blessing. Common to most people's experience was very
intense emotion, and they took this to be proof that God was touching
them. People seemed to receive an immediate sense of satisfaction, but
surely these feelings wouldn't last forever?

It all started at a church meeting. They were all gathered together
and the leader announced that everyone was going to be prayed for. Evan
wasn't averse to this. Prayers were a good thing, and why not pray for as
many people as possible? The instructions from the front to the prayer
team were to 'blow lightly onto people'. This was to signify the breath of
the Holy Spirit being breathed into individual lives. 'Fair enough,' Evan
thought, 'I can accept that.'

As he stood at the front and watched people blow on each other, all
kinds of strange things began to happen. Many fell flat on their backs,
others made funny noises, while some cried, and others laughed. Evan
noticed that everyone who had been prayed for was being obviously
affected in some way. Then it was his turn for prayer. He felt the breath
of a middle-aged man on his forehead. Nothing happened. He blew
again. Evan stood there quietly in the midst of the mayhem. It was OK,

he told himself, he didn't need to have a massive experience, he was quite happy.

The guy praying was obviously not. He seemed to need something to happen. Evan suddenly felt a push on his head. He thought, 'I'm not going to fall over, not unless God wants me to. Yes, everyone around me might be on the floor, but it doesn't mean I have to be.' The guy pushed on his head again. 'How insecure is this man?' Evan angrily thought. 'He won't stop until I'm on the floor.'

Evan used his head to push back against the man's hand. As his head rocked one way and then the other, his mind raced through a series of questions: Is this what is happening to everyone else? Is church really just a performance these days? How much of this stuff is real? This 'spiritual' moment had become purely a battle of wills. It was a kind of charismatic arm-wrestle. Evan was determined that there would be only one winner.

The stubborn pushing on his forehead continued, until Evan could handle it no longer. His whole body stiffened. He slowly lifted his head, opened his eyes and glared at the guy praying for him. In a composed but strong tone he said, 'If you don't believe in Jesus enough for him to make me fall over, then you can go and stuff yourself!' With that he turned and walked out.

The intensity and public nature of the event meant that this seed had been planted deep. Evan dwelt on the weirdness of the man's behaviour and it made him begin to wonder: 'If they were funny with me in that meeting, what else is manufactured?' Instead of giving some of the meetings and experiences the benefit of the doubt, Evan became more and more sceptical. One person would fall over, and then everyone else had to follow suit like religious dominoes. It was as if the noises and movement needed to get bigger and bigger to prove God was at work. He began to think people would go to any lengths in order for 'it' to happen. Evan's new-found mistrust of one guy was causing him to become cynical about everyone at church.

Though he didn't notice it during this period, he was choosing seats nearer and nearer the back of the church, until he was eventually slouching against the back wall. He chose to disconnect from meetings, rapidly becoming only a cynical observer with a deep scowl on his face. As he watched people 'receive', he let his thoughts run away with him: 'Why do they need to behave like this? It's almost like they have to have a bizarre experience, or somehow they will be regarded as less holy than the rest. It seems that if they make the biggest noise or fall over frequently, then they clearly love God the most!' Evan wasn't even sure if Mrs Ambrose – the youth leader he greatly respected – was being genuine. As he watched her laughing and shaking from the safety of the back row, he thought it all looked so fabricated. Either that or they are all suffering a mass delusion, he thought.

Evan began to wonder what the point of all this was. Surely there were better things to be doing? The tree of cynicism was growing fast and his observations caused branches to grow into new areas of his life. He started to question other things. Christians would say things like, 'God has told me to go to Outer Mongolia – so I'm leaving tomorrow', or 'Jesus is telling you to give up being a postman to deliver the gospel instead.' Evan would snigger under his breath, wondering how they knew for sure that God was saying such things. Shouldn't they prefix their comments with 'I think'? In a sarcastic tone he relayed some of his thoughts to a friend: 'Church is doing my head in. Everything has become about the individual, about *me* – Lord, come and bless me, sort me out and help me, do something special in my life this week. If I'm not touched, then what's the point in coming to church?' His friend's laughing agreement hardened his attitude further.

In his mind, 'they' were the ones being cynical, not him – he felt that they were manipulating God's power just to provide an experience. 'They' had to realize that God would move when he wanted to, not when they chose to engineer it. As far as he could see, God did not need a helping hand! Evan, however, was fine. He might not believe in God's people, but he believed in God. He had life sorted; it was everyone else who was confused.

The final nail in the coffin came on a trip to America. Evan and his family were visiting a massive church, and a famous television evangelist was taking to the stage that night. He was a healing 'specialist'. The family arrived early to get good seats. Evan drank in his surroundings. He was amazed at the wealth and the size of the building – there were luxurious seats and carpets in a huge arena seating over 5,000 people. They had arrived so early that the auditorium was still empty apart from a couple of men fiddling with microphones on the stage, which was illuminated by spotlights in front of the red velvet curtains. They nipped backstage as the audience began to pour in. Row after row of cinema-style chairs were filled with people from many ethnic groups and social backgrounds. Eventually a voice bellowed over the loud-speaker: 'Please find a seat quickly as the service is about to begin.'

The meeting seemed to be going well. People appeared to be being healed of various relatively minor injuries and illnesses. Then it was time for the main act. A guy in a wheelchair was rolled to the front by one of his friends. The mighty healer stepped forward, explaining to the audience that this gentleman had been paralysed from the neck down in a car accident a few years ago. He was simply going to ask God to heal the guy completely. As he started to pray, the wheelchair occupant began to move – slowly at first, but then the joints in his legs started to work together coherently. The healer asked the guy to try and stand up. He did. And then he walked! Everyone watching gasped – except for Evan. As the 'paralysed' man turned to face the crowd, Evan was absolutely convinced that the man he was staring at was one of the men who had nipped behind the curtain ninety minutes earlier. His sidekick had been pushing his wheelchair. Everyone stood and applauded, praising God at the tops of their voices with hands raised. Evan stayed wedged in his seat, his suspicious scowl reclaiming his face. If you were planning an event like this, it would make a perfect grand finale to the evening, wouldn't it? The coincidence of two blokes wearing exactly the same clothes with the same hair colour left him believing that his verdict was 'beyond reasonable doubt'.

Evan relayed his doubt and anger to his father. 'Why would they do that?' his father said. 'You can't be sure they did, son. You might have been imagining things.' He continued to dismiss it further: 'Anyway, you know God can move in great power. Whether he chose to tonight or not, we don't know, but we do know that he can.' Evan did agree with his father in part, but he was shaken. This scenario only served to fertilize his cynicism. He became critical of every so-called 'move of God', questioning every motive and watching Christians like a hawk for even the slightest hint of hypocrisy.

He descended into a 'prodigal period' where he wanted nothing to do with God or church. He focused his energies on playing football and religiously supporting his local football team.

Then one day, sitting in his bedroom, Evan realized he was tired. Tired of only reacting to what other people did. Tired of the constant critique of motives and methods. Tired of feeling the need to rate every preacher or worship leader. In the midst of all this, had he lost himself? He believed he was born to be a leader, but at the moment the most proactive thing he was doing was choosing which TV channel to watch. He realized that if he wasn't happy with the state of the church, then the place to be was inside it, making it better. He could never do that from the outside.

His re-engagement seemed to switch off his selective memory, as he suddenly remembered a time when he had been prayed for (before all the craziness started) and he had fallen to the floor like a feather. He knew it was real because the guy hadn't laid a finger on him. And as he had lain there on the ground, an overwhelming sense of peace had come over him. He knew Jesus was real because he had seen amazing things happen when he had prayed. For example, as a nine-year-old he had asked God to remove a verruca from a lad's foot, and then watched in amazement as it disappeared. He knew only God could do that.

Shaun isn't at the back of the church any more. In fact, today he's at the front. He now works for Youth For Christ and speaks at many youth events. It had been easy to shout at the guy who had tried to push him over because he wasn't the one who had to do the praying. It had been easy to sit on the sidelines and criticize. But now he's a bit older and the roles are reversed: the responsibility is on his shoulders. Evan is delivering his message to some young people and now he needs God to come through. He needs him to do something radical – to prove to the folk in the room that Jesus is real.

He smiles to himself as he realizes the new state of play. He remembers his old scornful thoughts: 'They shouldn't be making things happen. If God wants to move, he will do it in his own way.' But they are now mixed with some new ones: 'What if he doesn't move? They won't come to one of these meetings again. For this to go down in history as a good youth meeting, surely something tangible needs to happen?' Evan feels challenged. 'There are two sides to every story,' he concludes. He has learnt to love the church and is discovering how it feels to sit on the vulnerable side, longing for God to move. He may have made the journey from cynical commentator in the stands to determined player on the pitch, and his maturity may be opening his eyes to see a much bigger picture, but he's still human.

The battle between present and past lingers in Evan's mind as he draws the talk to a close. He watches young people respond and adds one last conscious point to his message:

'Whether or not you see God or feel him do anything in your life tonight, don't rely on that as proof that he is real. Please don't compare your experience with your friend's, because God may choose to work in you in a way that is totally different. Above all, hold onto your faith and remember that "faith is being sure of what we hope for and certain of what we do not see."'

Now, that is a seed worth planting.

They think it's all over...

A deeply troubled man wearing a heavy hood sneaks into an internet café somewhere between the Garden of Gethsemane and the High Priest's courtyard. To his online devotees, Blog Peter (artistpreviouslyknownassimon@fish.co.uk) has become essential daily reading. The blog begins:

So what was the point of all that?

I try to be loyal, but it seems like I got it wrong again. It's so unfair, because I always do exactly what he tells me. At Cana he asks me to do something that made me the butt of all the jokes, but I did it. (Mind you, I was laughing cheerily pretty soon afterwards.) I follow his fishing instructions to the letter, even though he hasn't so much as caught a goldfish in his life. And I go on secret missions for donkeys for him, using strange passwords. I do whatever he asks of me. I really do. Maybe that was the problem tonight. He didn't ask.

Tonight reminded me of another time when he was ranting on about all this death and resurrection stuff. I tried to be a loyal spin doctor, looking out for his best interests, so I pulled him aside from the gathered crew. I had a quiet word, explaining that all this death talk wasn't good for morale, and that we needed to 'sex up' the language a bit to get a few more people on board. I suggested that we use phrases like 'the implementation of the next phase of the stimulus package for Israel'. People would vote for that. Nobody wants to play for a captain who's heading for an early bath. I won't tell you the language he used, but he told me in no uncertain terms that we would be running the campaign *his* way.

He had mentioned the death and resurrection thing again recently, but I guess I thought it was metaphorical, or at least many months into the future. I'm becoming increasingly worried that he was serious. He has some sort of death wish. Which is majorly disappointing because things were just starting to go really well. He got a hero's welcome a few days ago, and I reckon if he gave the word, the people would rise up and do some serious damage to the Romans. Recently 'the disciple who loves himself' has been getting closer and closer to him, so I wasn't as sure as I was before, but I seriously thought I had first shout at being Prime Minister of the new Government.

I don't understand how I could have got the wrong end of the stick. We had this secret war cabinet in an upper room which finished with him telling us that we would sit on thrones in his kingdom. Good motivational stuff. It all had a sense of grave finality about it and there was an obvious change of tactics afoot. In contrast to previous instructions, this time we were told to go out with cash, bags and swords at the ready. 'Game on,' we thought. As we were leaving, the lads kept making cock-a-doodle-doo noises to wind me up. The swines! I think Jesus was just having a laugh about all that, though. I'm the Rock, after all.

We went out to Jesus' favourite prayer spot, the Mount of Olives. (Imagine if it really was a mountain of olives – yummy... Sorry, I'm digressing.) Jesus asked us to pray, but it was getting late and by this stage we were all pretty knackered. The last few days have been intense, to say the least. He said, 'Get up and pray so that you will not fall into temptation,' I didn't think I was likely to fall, but I hadn't counted on what happened next.

Turns out Judas has shopped Jesus to the other side! I knew he'd been looking shifty recently but I presumed he was just feeling the pressure like the rest of us. He couldn't wait for the moment when we were going to do the proper revolution bit. He'd even come up with a pile of slogans for the people to chant. ('Jesus' 12 – Romans nil' was my personal favourite.) I'd thought he was just getting pre-match anxiety. I'd like to know how much the traitor got.

He arrived with the temple guard to arrest Jesus, and we thought, 'This is it! This is where it gets bloody.' The lads shouted at Jesus, 'Should we strike with our swords?', but I didn't need an invitation. This was my chance to show my loyalty and leadership. I went straight for the High Priest's servant's head, but he swayed out of the way, and I just got his ear. Those who have ears, let them hear, eh? Things were about to get frantic when Jesus suddenly said, 'No more of this!' Everyone froze. He had such authority in his voice. He stretched out his hand and did the fastest piece of plastic surgery I've ever seen. I felt absolutely minute. Yet again I had jumped in before everyone else, and got told off for it. I just can't seem to help myself. I've always been like this. I used to get the fiercest looks from my mother when we had guests over, and I would pipe up with something inappropriate during dinner like, 'So you don't smell of fish as much as your husband, Mrs Zebedee.'

Seriously, though. I'm gutted. And confused. Jesus was meant to lead us to victory and now he's been arrested. Maybe he has some clever plan that he couldn't even tell us about.

Right, I've got to go. They've taken Jesus over to the High Priest's place. He'll need some moral support.

Prelude to a denial

It's fun to speculate around the thoughts and feelings of our friend Peter whom we have journeyed with, and there may be some morsels of truth there, but I honestly don't think that's how Peter's blog would have read that night. Actually, I'm not sure he would have been able to communicate with anyone at all, because he'd just had a red carpet pulled out from under him. His assumptions had been dashed, and his mind must have been in turmoil. There would have been no time for comedy. He was desperately trying to reconcile what had just occurred with the things that Jesus had said would happen, cross-referencing old speeches and one-liners in his head. And all this was happening as he ploughed through the darkness with John, trying to follow at a frightened distance. The man whom he had pledged to give his life for hadn't given him that chance, and the man whom he loved so dearly had been taken by those who certainly didn't. We all know what happened next, but I've never fully understood how this wonderful, brave and at times stupid man called Peter could suddenly turn into an evasive politician around a charcoal fire, being 'economic with the truth'. I know I could fold under the pressure, but it just doesn't seem to fit *his* character. We need to chisel deeper to what is going on inside the mind and heart of the rock.

Much as I'd love to think that I am immune to outside influence, I see peer pressure in operation all the time in my life. I have, however, noticed something about its appearance. It only works because a doubt has been subtly planted in my mind that leaves some 'wiggle room'. If I am utterly convinced of something, then I can usually stand my ground, but if even a hint of a question-mark begins to appear, then I'm in trouble. We shouldn't be surprised at this, of course. This is how everything went wrong in the first place. It wasn't a bold statement from the snake in the garden of Eden, but a subtle question: 'Is that *really* what God said about the tree?' Doubt about the truth was planted for the first time, and a huge doubt tree grew very quickly to provide cover for what Adam and Eve wanted to do.

Knowing this transforms how we think about Peter's denial in the High Priest's courtyard. His worldview has been shattered. The man who he thought was the Messiah had been captured without putting up a fight. When he had tried to put up a fight for him, he had got scolded again! In his fear he was beginning to doubt what this whole three-year adventure had been about. Jesus had failed to meet Peter's expectations. Someone who had been about to start ruling over the new kingdom of Israel shouldn't have been trudging off in chains.

Peter wasn't the only one whose expectations weren't being met. Some couldn't believe he was the Messiah purely because a few years previously he had been fixing their chairs or making them a table. It's hard to overplay the desperation with which the Jews were awaiting a Messiah, but their desires and God's plans weren't necessarily intersecting. This has resonances with Evan's story of questionable healings and gravity-aided ministry, where he met many Christians who were relying on their own ideas of power, rather than God's. Some of them were building earthly kingdoms. It's so easy to do, and it's so easy to find good reasons to justify your actions.

But the rest of the Jews weren't experiencing the personal crisis that Peter was experiencing at this moment. He was gloriously human, and Peter believed he would have some serious earthly influence when the new kingdom kicked in. This dynamic operates even today in elections. Those who back a presidential or prime ministerial candidate, forming his campaign team when in opposition, are usually rewarded with plum jobs if and when the candidate gets into power. The disciples were not immune to this perceived patronage. For Peter personally, a massive turn-around had occurred. There was a big psychological difference between planning for next week as your first week of office in the new free kingdom of Israel, and strategizing about how to survive as the right-hand man of Jerusalem's 'Most Wanted'. He wasn't prepared for this. It was all too confusing. Perhaps Jesus simply wasn't who he said he was?

How often do our moments of doubt and frustration follow on from times when Jesus has failed to meet the expectations that we put on him? There are times when he does not deliver on the day that we told him he should. Or there are times when the delivery has been something different to what we, the consumer, requested! I fear that the times when I am disappointed by God could be more accurately described as being disappointed by Santa.

Brian had been praying that his most recent foster family would work out, and found himself disappointed with God when it didn't. That was just enough doubt to start a chain reaction, though the bust-up with the family also made him doubt whether he had changed that much.

The same is true of Peter. He wasn't only doubting Jesus. He was also doubting himself. He had spent the last minutes running like a coward in the dark, instead of standing beside his Master. Pride can come before a fall, but often I have found that a sense of inadequacy can do the tripping just as successfully. It can make you think, 'Well, what's the point? I muck everything up anyway... When I try to do right, it goes wrong, so why bother?' Into this swirl of confusion came the question: 'You're one of Jesus' followers, aren't you?'

> Then seizing him, they led him away and took him into the house of the high priest. Peter followed at a distance. But when they had kindled a fire in the middle of the courtyard and had sat down together, Peter sat down with them. A servant girl saw him seated there in the firelight. She looked closely at him and said, 'This man was with him.'
>
> But he denied it. 'Woman, I don't know him,' he said.
>
> A little later someone else saw him and said, 'You also are one of them.'
>
> 'Man, I am not!' Peter replied.
>
> About an hour later another asserted, 'Certainly this fellow was with him, for he is a Galilean.'
>
> Peter replied, 'Man, I don't know what you're talking about!' Just as he was speaking, the cock crowed. The Lord turned and looked straight at

Peter. Then Peter remembered the word the Lord had spoken to him: 'Before the cock crows today, you will disown me three times.' And he went outside and wept bitterly. (Luke 22:54–62)

In his response Peter may have been more honest than we or he would care to admit. In those moments of failure and frustration, we do often begin to doubt if, in fact, we are followers of this Jesus. We fool ourselves that because of the situation we find ourselves in, we've been kidding ourselves that we can manage this God stuff. We start to cling onto what we can taste, touch and feel rather than what we know deep down to be true. This questioning is often just large enough to provide the cover we need for our moments of sin and betrayal. When Peter said, 'I do not know the man', he was perhaps again speaking more truth than we give him credit for. He was thinking, 'I thought I knew him, but he's obviously not who I thought he was.'

It's at moments like this that I am reminded that Jesus came to save me from my sin. I like to think that he came to save me from a whole pile of other things as well, but *he* never promised that. *I* decided that. I decided that as a Christian I should be saved from living in an estate, that I should be saved from terminal illness, that I should be saved from war zones, and that I should be saved from difficult relationships. He never promised me these things, yet I blame him and use my frustrations as excuses for betrayal. Evan knew what it was like to use his frustrations as a cover for his cynicism. He began to doubt whether the whole God thing was real. For some time he wouldn't have anything to do with God, as a kind of protest. The problem with this kind of protest is that it's directed at someone who, at that point, you don't believe exists, so the whole plan doesn't really hold together.

Silent treatment

All the way through this journey Peter had been engaging his mouth before putting his brain into gear. That nasty gear-crunching noise had been heard during the transfiguration experience, during some foot-washing, and other random moments of Jesus' preaching. It had been a steep learning curve during which Peter hadn't seemed too worried about going out on a limb to see how much weight it could take before it invariably came crashing down. But all that had changed. The most striking difference now was not perhaps his three-fold denial, but his lack of words when there was space and time to stand up for Jesus at the High Priest's house. Surely if ever there was a time for brain-free, over-excited, loyal, passionate oratory, then this was it. Surely Jesus needed a defender to vouch for his good intentions and the amazing fruit of his ministry. But no. Scared, confused silence reigned.

When we hide away from the truth, those silent moments can become longer and more dangerous as our shame about recent activities or thoughts prevents us from returning to the one who would actually sort it all out. Helen spent months like this in hiding, knowing that she had met Jesus, but confused by her own continuing ability to self-destruct. None of it seemed to add up. This gets to the heart of why it is so important for us to get inside the life of Peter. I fear that we have been guilty of only providing 'success' role models to young people, in our enthusiasm to woo them into the kingdom. We are less likely to speak about times of struggle and doubt, and therefore these things are not normalized into a young person's perception of what the journey of faith should look like. If what they are experiencing then doesn't compute with the image that has been portrayed, then the baby may well go out with the bath-water. It's as if, in a traumatic moment, the screen of their life freezes, and instead of patiently waiting for the computer to start functioning again, they head straight for the 'off' button. Thankfully, someone like Phil was able to hold onto what he knew to be true in the midst of his trauma.

When I am representing YFC on radio discussion programmes, what surprises other contributors is that we respond to the needs of young people. Sometimes people believe that we simply assault a group of young people with our agenda. Local YFC workers always work by building relationships with young people, listening to their stories, and understanding their concerns. This creates a context for youth workers to honestly share their own stories, which often shatter any illusions that life will be rosy from the moment you become a Christian.

Shame

There is no record in the gospels of Peter being present at the crucifixion. He was still hiding then. Relatively unknown disciples were left to look after Jesus' body for burial. Where was he hiding? How could the rock on which Jesus would build his church have missed the moment which that church would continually speak, write and sing about for hundreds of years?

We're much too good at shame. We all know the feeling of being unable to look someone in the eye when we know we have wronged them. Multiply that by about a thousand and perhaps you start to get a picture of how Peter must have been feeling. I love the fact that for much of his life he was quite literally a 'promising failure', but for now he just felt like a failure. Where do you go from there? And how do you help someone who is there?

There are no easy answers, but Helen's story underlines how being in the presence of Jesus starts to peel the layers of shame back off. Only once these layers get stripped back can we be honest with God and with each other. It is a privilege to be involved in many of the gatherings organized by local YFC centres. Typically, young people gather from all over a town to worship, pray together and be taught. It is often during these gatherings, where there is space for simply resting in God's presence (sometimes connected to times of sung worship), that young people feel safe to confess, unload, laugh, minister, reveal,

cry, and communicate honestly with their God. In the safety of being uncondi-
tionally loved, all kinds of grace can pour into dark crevices of the soul, be they
memories or present issues. I often start an evening by saying, 'Tonight we're
going to stop for long enough to let ourselves be loved.'

For Peter, you get the feeling that he had been in a limbo-like state until he
was once again in the presence of Jesus. Jesus had appeared to the disciples,
but fleetingly, and not like in the old days. Besides, there was still no sign of a
revolution. Had Peter been sleeping properly? Had he been talking to anyone
about it? Had he honestly expressed his frustration and confusion to anybody? I
don't think so. I think he was numb. I think he was on autopilot. He'd gone back
to the one thing he knew and understood, which was fishing. When we don't
want to face our internal struggles, like Brian didn't want to, we seek out what
is most familiar to us for subconscious comfort. For Brian it was the estate. For
Peter it was the sea of Galilee.

Helen's gut-fuelled run towards the front of that meeting for her restoration moment reminds me of Peter's swim/wade to the beach in John 21. When
they reached their destinations they both found what they needed, even though
they didn't know what they needed. Here's Peter's story.

Not drowning, but wading

So he went back to what he knew, and it seems as if the disciples were in a similar state of mind. He was still the only one who would get up and do anything,
though. 'I'm going out to fish,' he announced. 'We'll go with you,' came the reply.
You can imagine them all sitting in a lakeside tavern staring at the ceiling or
playing cards. Nobody had the nerve to bring up the subject of Jesus. Nobody
was quite sure what to believe, and certainly nobody knew what to do next.
Better to not mention it.

I suspect Peter's idea was the first positive suggestion that they'd heard in a while. They must have leapt at the idea. Unfortunately, they discovered that even their fishing had returned to its pre-Jesus disappointing standard. They worked all night and caught nothing. This is sounding familiar. First thing in the morning, there was some bloke standing on the shore rubbing salt in their wounds: 'Haven't you caught any fish?' he cheekily asked. I love the way that John's Gospel describes their carefully thought-out and long-winded response: 'No!' they answered. I suspect other phrases such as, 'Do you think we'd still be out here if we had?' or 'What's it to you?' or 'What are you doing up at this time anyway?' would have sprung to mind if they had been more awake, or if their mood had been more upbeat. 'No!' – I can imagine their slumped shoulders as they mumbled it as one. Then the stranger began to push his luck, offering fishing advice. They remembered that the last person to do that had been Jesus, so this bloke couldn't be all that bad. They followed his advice and lo and behold, it was *Miracle Catch 2 – The Sequel*.

John was the first to put two and two together, and recognize that it was Jesus. D'oh! Peter needed no second invitation. He threw his 'outer garment' on and jumped into the water. Again, this was not a thought-out response to Jesus. This was an organic, knee-jerk, honest reaction from the Rock. He was compelled. His Master was back! He didn't want to waste a moment. Particularly entertaining is the fact that Peter put clothes on for his swim to the beach. I'm sure he just wanted to be decent before the Lord. The chaos continued, as the disciples followed him in the boat, towing their massive catch behind them. Soon Peter was back in the boat again after Jesus suggested cooking some of their catch right now. This was even though he was already grilling away with the fish that he had caught/created/transported/replicated (delete as appropriate). In the short time he'd been away, had Jesus forgotten how many disciples he had, and under-bargained on the fish front? Was he trying to underline the point that he would 'catch' the first converts, but it would be their job to 'fish' for the rest? Or was the gospel-writer John simply having some fun and enjoying the randomness of his last chapter? The last theory begins to look slightly more likely when you finish verse 11. It says this:

> Simon Peter climbed aboard and dragged the net ashore. It was full of large fish, 153, but even with so many the net was not torn.

One hundred and fifty three! I know that's a lot of fish, but can you believe the detail? We had 'The Feeding the Five Thousand', not 'The Feeding of the 5013'. Later we will have three thousand added to the church at Pentecost, not the 2,987 who actually filled in response forms and took a tract. What's going on? Why the sudden preciseness?

And even more worrying, who took the time to count them when their Lord and Saviour had just reappeared for what might have been the last time ever. Can you imagine it?

With excitement they shouted, 'Thaddeus! Come over here! Jesus is back! He is risen and he's here with us now in person!!!!'

'Shush! I'm counting! Darn, you've made me lose count again... 1, 2, 3, 4...' Maybe Thaddeus liked his fish. He was probably the one who invented the car stickers.

But Jesus called them all together for breakfast, and he 'took the bread and gave it to them'. All doubt was gone. This was Jesus' calling-card, without a doubt.

Restoration

Remember that intense *emblepo* gaze of Jesus which first fixed Peter on the seashore, and then again in the courtyard? Well, when I asked how you help restore someone who is feeling like a failure, there is your answer. Get them into Jesus' presence, and hope that they sit still for long enough to hear him ask, 'Do you truly love me?' There will be a moment where once again they can meet his *emblepo* gaze, and realize that they are *still* loved. He simply won't find the reasons that we'll often find to not express our love.

Tim bumped into Brian a few times after the burglary. Once the bravado of the moment had subsided, there was one thing Brian could never do. Look him straight in the eye. He would mostly look downward and shuffle his feet, or look wistfully into the near distance, but their souls didn't get that chance that eyeballs provide to connect again.

What needs stressing to any young person, as it was stressed to Lewis, and as Jesus made clear to Peter, is that whatever has happened is not a disqualification from ministry. Jesus actually incorporated this assertion into his restorative words with his triple instruction. As he allowed Peter to be reconciled, he told him to 'Feed my lambs', 'Take care of my sheep' and 'Feed my sheep'. It certainly wasn't a golden handshake. This encounter at the end of John's Gospel is surely one of the most poignant in all of scripture. We have followed this relationship all the way from its inception to now. We know how much each man had invested in the other. We know the heartbreak that Peter had experienced and the pain that he had caused Jesus. Yet Jesus went out of his way to create a safe place for Peter to be made whole again. He wove the threads together to create a beautiful fabric. They were on the seashore, where they had first met. They were eating fish – a meal they must have shared many times. And a charcoal fire was burning. Our sense of smell is one of the most evocative of the senses. We strongly associate smells with specific memories, whether that be a pine forest, or a sick baby, or a new car. The smoky smell of this fire immediately took Peter back to the High Priest's courtyard, where he had warmed himself around a charcoal fire. He was right back in the moment, able to speak truth directly to the lies he had told that night. Similarly, as Lewis encountered God's grace, he was able to speak truth into the relationship situation where he had been simply lying to himself. Jesus made sure that Peter and Lewis would both be leading not from a place of pride but from a place of brokenness. As Oscar Wilde said, 'Except by a broken heart, how else could the Lord Christ enter in.'

None of us could manage life without our own daily versions of what took place on that beach that morning. Many of our denials will be sins of omission rather than sins of commission. Perhaps our charcoal fire is the sound and light of a humming photocopier, in the office chat where we've stepped back from owning Jesus as Lord of our lives. Perhaps our charcoal fire is the smell of a football changing-room, where we've pressed our back further into the wall rather than stand up for Jesus. Perhaps our charcoal fire is the sound of pop-up advertisements on the websites that we shouldn't have been anywhere near. Perhaps our charcoal fire is the smell of the hospital ward where we jettisoned ethics for speed. You may want to take some time in the near future to revisit that place and just rest there awhile with Jesus. Ask for his forgiveness. Receive his grace. Let him restore those memories. He'll have got there before you. And he's cooking...

Peer pressure

Shaun's story highlights one of the key issues and opportunities in youth culture. On only his first day at secondary school he realized what he was going to need to do to survive. People will always revere and follow those who are 'edgy'. There is a magnetism about their difference. The calculation our minds perform is that to have the nerve to wear those different clothes or stand up to that authority, they must have a confidence in who they are and what they believe. We think there may be something in this, and we follow. Peer pressure is created. Our disappointment, as in Jemima's case, occurs when we find out that there isn't a pot of gold at the end of the rainbow, and the attitude that was so alluring is only skin deep. There's often no soul to the unique exterior. So whether it's music, fashion or bullying, young people get sucked into a vicious cycle of trying to 'out-edge' each other, stretching the edge of the circle further and further from whom they really are at the centre.

But herein lies the opportunity. Increasingly, those who are truly 'edgy' in their teens are those who are living counter-culturally – giving their lives in the service of their communities, campaigning on behalf of the developing world, and radically loving people when it would be much easier to walk on by. These people make others look up and follow.

Peter experienced this with Jesus. He and the disciples were the biggest show in town. Everyone wanted to get close to Jesus. Everyone wanted to hear what he had to say. If the story of the Galileans was being played out in our century, you would have a queue of people wanting to have their photograph taken with Jesus. People jump on bandwagons pretty quickly and everyone wants to be ahead of the game in knowing the next 'rising star'. The fantastic thing is that following these new followers is not a fruitless task. The man whom they are following had style *and* substance. His life wasn't driven by insecurity and the need for affirmation and power. His actions were driven by the pure core of who he was. That sounds like the sort of man I want to follow. His name is Jesus.

There were two guys at my school who weren't even close to the edge. There was no one checking out their tastes in music or fashion. The fact that they wore NHS spectacles wasn't making life easy for them. Neither was the fact that they were identical twins. Neither was the fact that the Proclaimers were pretty big at that time. They were often the laughing stock of the sports field. When one of them shied away from making a tackle on the rugby pitch, the PE teacher asked him, 'Do you want me to give you white gloves, so you can just wave him through?'

There were a few of us in our year at school who would have put our heads above the parapet and said that we were Christians. The lack of numbers led to lack of confidence and lack of activity. The twins, Trevor and Colin, kept suggesting that we should meet together to pray at lunchtimes. They seemed to think that that might be the way forward. My activist self failed to see the use in hiding away for half of lunchtime every Tuesday and Friday in a maths classroom at the top of the building. But Trevor and Colin started doing it faithfully. For months there would only be three or four people at most. I dismissed it as having your head in the clouds when your feet should be on the ground (and there weren't any girls there). But people started coming. Eventually they won me over. The topics for prayer and people's names would be written on a big rotating blackboard, and people got stuck into praying in small groups. Within two years there were almost a hundred people meeting there regularly. It became the lifeblood of anything that was happening. People were coming to faith left, right and centre. Only looking back on it now does it seem remarkable, because at the time it felt normal and obvious. The Christian events became the ones to be seen at. Positive peer pressure was operating in a massive way. The group got involved with local churches and social action projects. People in the town were noticing that there was an energy and life about this ever-growing horde. I will never forget the day when the list of prefects was put up on a noticeboard. I counted through the names. Exactly three quarters of the prefects were Christians.

It is still happening in countless schools today. YFC have the privilege of connecting with 450 schools in England, Scotland and Wales. Workers are involved in many, many ways from supporting Christian groups, to taking assemblies, PSHE lessons and RE lessons, and delivering pastoral support. Through the government's new plans for extended schools, this involvement is going to increase significantly. My four years at Portadown College taught me to keep an eye on what is invisible as well as what is visible. In following everyone else's eyes to the visible edges, I missed the guys who were truly on the edge – the guys who started a quiet revolution from a maths classroom.

New Peter

What a day! The day the church became more than just a youth group. The day all the waiting became worth it. The day that had every blogger, TV reporter and newspaper editor searching for words to describe what had happened. The day that caused emergency committee meetings in the highest ranks of Jerusalem's rulers. The day when 6,000 Pharisees began to look like not such a big number.

This couldn't be pigeon-holed as simply a symbolic act. Some had done that with the crucifixion of Jesus, allowing themselves the intellectual space to debate its meaning and draw their own less radical conclusions. This time, miraculous things had occurred within earshot of thousands of eye-witnesses who were from so many different places that a conspiracy theory was simply implausible.

Was it really possible that a man who had been hiding away in fear was behind all this? People without an education like this lot usually made their mark with swords and fists, not with oratory and supernatural occurrences. But 'Ah,' they said, 'they have been with Jesus.' The shekels were beginning to drop.

One abiding fact stands out for me from the accounts of this day. Though Peter had evidently been transformed, the content of what he said was what he had known to be true for some time. It had not changed. He had not received any extra great revelation. He had simply been emboldened to speak what he knew, and to rely on someone else's strength to do it. The words did flow in a way that they had never flowed before. He hadn't had speech-writing staff to train him. He hadn't had public-speaking training in use of the diaphragm or how to use a dramatic pause. Something just clicked.

So how had Peter the fisherman – confused, scared and weary – become Peter the mass evangelist? As he stood there preaching on that day, I imagine him hearing the echoes of Jesus words' in his ears: 'I will make you fishers of men.' I imagine him, in his mind's eye, casting a great net out across the gathered crowd. He tossed it far and wide. His words drew the stragglers into the net, and by some invisible force they were not wriggling or fighting like they normally would. Then, with a precision which he had never known before, he drew the net in over the side of the platform on which he stood. He smiled. It was *Miracle Catch III – Return of the Master*!

This was a new time. Jesus was still healing, only now he was healing through the hands of Peter. Jesus was still speaking, only now he was speaking through the mouth of Peter. You get the sense that Peter was beginning to realize this. The reason for this transformation lies at the start of Acts. Let's go back there.

We make a mistake if we believe that everything changed just because of one spiritual experience. Obviously this was a massive factor, but there was also a wider picture. The disciples' confidence was building. They had had forty days of sporadic precious interaction with their risen saviour. Things seemed to be back on track again. Jesus seems pretty specific with his instructions about not leaving Jerusalem. Something big was going down in the next few days. What on earth would that be? Eventually the party was over, and Jesus returned to heaven. But just before he left there was time for one last question. It's almost like something from an ice-breaker game. If you had one question to ask your saviour before he ascended to heaven, what would it be? From the myriad of options that may be ticking through your head, the disciples managed to pick one that shows that their new-found confidence wasn't yet aligned with new-found understanding:

> So when they met together, they asked him, 'Lord, are you at this time going to restore the kingdom to Israel?' (Acts 1:6)

They were still asking about restoring the kingdom to Israel. They still thought that the kingdom was coming in a political sense. It really wasn't until the great big download in Jerusalem that they realized that it was a spiritual kingdom. Jesus kindly decided not to go for the big rebuke with his last words, but instead steered them gently to the real point:

> It is not for you to know the times or dates the Father has set by his own authority. But you will receive power when the Holy Spirit comes on you; and you will be my witnesses in Jerusalem, and in all Judea and Samaria, and to the ends of the earth. (Acts 1:7–8)

Jesus headed skyward, and Peter assumed the mantle of leadership pretty much immediately. We talk about people having God-given authority, but could ever the phrase have been applied more accurately and specifically than to Peter at this moment?

His authority had obviously been developing. He had been studying scripture and was keen to lead, not simply for the sake of it, but because he believed the scriptures must be fulfilled. Read Acts chapter 1. This was now a man on a mission. Point 1 on the agenda was the selection of a replacement for Judas. Confidence was still building. They now had a mission statement, and an organization that is winding down or cowering away doesn't bother with replacing staff.

And so to Pentecost. We now speak of Pentecost as if it was the 'feast of the Holy Spirit', forgetting that the original purpose of this feast was to commemorate the completion of the grain harvest. Its distinguishing feature was the offering of 'two leavened loaves' made from the new corn of the completed harvest, which, with two lambs, were waved before the Lord as a thanks offering. The fact that God chose to send his Spirit at this time underlines again the smooth continuum between the old and new covenants. The big story was continuing to hold together.

The Holy Spirit moved spectacularly and the disciples formed the first ever team of United Nations interpreters. Except no one had any ear-pieces in their

ears. Something very special was going on. The curse of Babel was being broken. God was letting the world know that finally Israel was stepping into its destiny to be a light to the Gentiles. This message was going global. It would take a
strong man to stand up amidst the mayhem and make sense of it all. God was
saying, 'Here's one I prepared earlier.' Everything in Peter's life had been building up to this moment. I feel I've been privileged to sit on the roller-coaster with
him. Now I just want to sit and listen. Go Peter! Have a read of Acts chapter 2.

Talking

If you analyse Peter's first three sermons, you find something very interesting.
His first sermon in Acts 2 was basically an explanation of what had taken place,
throwing in some quotes from David and Joel. He started off by story-telling,
which is how most of the YFC volunteers start off their preaching lives. He was
relaying what he had experienced. Nobody can take your own experience away
from you. There is nothing more powerful than someone telling their own story.
It's what Jemima did at school, and it's what Shaun does in prisons. There is
something inherently powerful and, importantly, disarming about story-telling.
We forget facts but we remember stories. Jesus only ever used theological
words after he had fleshed them out by sharing an experience. A great example
is at the end of the story of Zaccheus when he says, 'Salvation has come to this
house.' He has just remarkably demonstrated what salvation is, and he gives it
a name.

This is a key aspect of speaking training within YFC. In this post-modern
age, if you simply present someone with what you claim is truth, they can only
do one of two things with it. Accept it or reject it. Without providing people with
any context, the chances are it will be rejected. We encourage folks to create a
context for the truth before inserting it. This can be done through story, humour
and emotion. You talk about things that people understand before you talk about

things that they don't. If they can agree with you on some of the early stuff, it's more likely that they will begin to agree with you later on. People won't respond to a solution until they agree with you on what the problem is.

Peter's second sermon, in Acts 3, arose as a response to his most famous miracle, which gave him some good material to work off, explaining the kafuffle that had been caused. It was only really when he got to his third sermon, in Acts 4, that he fully knew the promise of Jesus in Luke 21:13–15 coming true:

> This will result in your being witnesses to them. But make up your mind not to worry beforehand how you will defend yourselves. For I will give you words and wisdom that none of your adversaries will be able to resist or contradict.

It was at this point that Peter truly experienced total supernatural inspiration. He left his listeners speechless. They knew this eloquence was surely impossible for someone who had not studied. At this point his tongue really was 'the pen of a ready writer'. What is even more amazing is that Peter was standing in the same courtyard where he had denied Jesus. He now had the courage to preach about him in the light of day, whereas previously he couldn't even admit to knowing him in the cover of darkness.

The point I'm trying to make is that in terms of preaching, the building-blocks for Peter were actually pretty simple. There was no rocket science involved. If you analyse Peter's preaching you can see that he stuck to a pretty specific pattern. This is of vital importance in encouraging young people to see that what Peter achieved is possible today also. Peter didn't have any exclusive magic dust. Even the apostle Paul knew that he couldn't convince people merely with well-crafted words:

My message and my preaching were not with wise and persuasive words, but with a demonstration of the Spirit's power, so that your faith might not rest on men's wisdom, but on God's power.   (1 Corinthians 2:4–5)

People's attention is grabbed by the supernatural. It was in the first century AD and it still is now. There. I said it. I'm not ashamed of it. We'd like to think that we're more sophisticated than that, but we're not. People's heads will still be turned by a demonstration of the Spirit's power. And I wonder if that's why people like Peter, Shaun and Tim seem to see inexplicable 'coincidences' occurring in their lives. They have not yet been tied down by the shackles of cynicism and 'experience'. They still have the faith to believe that what Jesus said he will do, he will do.

Most young people don't want intellectual discussion and boxes to tick. Deep down they want a cause they can cheer for that comes from their gut. They don't care if they can't really put it into words. That's why so many people are obsessed with sporting teams. It's one of the few areas of life where people feel free to express themselves. In that context they can express utter excitement and happiness, but also searing cynicism and depression. Something is happening that goes way beyond mind to heart and soul. Where along the line did the church give up its territory to sport? Again, have we something to learn from the enthusiasm of young people who will scream and bounce and roar for their God, and give up their summer holidays for a cause that is so much bigger than them?

The remarkable change that we have seen in Peter, Jemima and John is the same change that I have had the privilege of seeing replicated in the hundreds of young people who work with British Youth For Christ. There is an attractiveness and confidence about these young people. They have grown up on the same estates as their peers. They are not better educated than them. They are not more talented than them. What makes them different is that, like Peter, they have heard and responded to the call of a man who sees their true self. It has given them a cause and a hope which is turning a generation hiding under a hoodie into a generation that is desperate to show the love of their leader Jesus to a hurting world. You might say that I'm exaggerating, but I'm talking about tens of thousands of young people. And that's a lot when you think that it only takes a couple of ASBO candidates to turn hundreds of column inches negative. I just want people to hear the whole story.

All around the UK they are learning what Jesus taught Peter, and teaching it to us by their lives. They are leading. And they are learning that the true place of a leader is on their knees, holding a towel, wiping the feet of the world.

As my boss Roy Crowne says, 'This isn't about making bad people good. This is about making dead people come alive.' My prayer is that more and more people won't turn towards the church and see an accusing finger pointing in their direction, but they'll turn towards the church and see a people so uncontrollably alive that they want to plug into the same socket.

You'll see this life and service in our final travelling companion on this journey – Anthony Brown.

11 Arrival

Anthony

Every day across planet earth, its six billion inhabitants interact with each other. Some will meet face to face. Some will talk on the phone. Some will communicate via the internet. Five per cent will be speaking English, just over five per cent will be speaking Spanish and more than fifteen per cent will be speaking Mandarin. Others will not talk to anyone at all, perhaps due to geographical separation, or broken relationships. There is, however, another group – those who will interact with many people in the course of a day, but come to the end of it feeling that they have not connected with any of them. They do not feel that anyone has 'opened up' to them in a way that speaks of trust and intimacy, but perhaps more importantly, they feel that their story has not been heard with the sacred listening it deserves.

Something told me that Anthony Brown was one such person. His story and my story intersected over the course of a few days, so I make no apology for the fact that this is my story too. I'm afraid there's only so much I can tell you about his. When we met, Anthony spoke of the role that he had eked out for himself as a loner. Even though he was only fourteen years old, he had a strange sense of foreboding that what he was experiencing now would be similar to the rest of his days. He was caught in the tension of wanting to be known and understood, but desperately trying to avoid the rejection that came crashing down on him with another failed attempt. There was no easy way of saying it. Anthony was not cool. We met Anthony during a week that our Youth For Christ band, TVB, spent in his town. As was our routine, we performed songs and took classes in schools all around the area, inviting the young people we met to a big concert on the Friday night.

Anthony was a diligent young man whom you couldn't define by the group that he hung around with because, in short, there wasn't one. His hair always had the look of someone who was pretending to not care about its appearance, but secretly did. But one thing more than anything else stood out about Anthony. His height. He was described by many people as a 'gentle giant'. The problem is that when you're taller than everyone else in your year group, there is quite literally nowhere to hide. You don't need to have a degree in youth work to work out that this alliance of gentleness and extreme height didn't score Anthony too many points in the playground league tables. He was easy pickings for the school bullies. The school playground is where so much of our learned behaviour emanates. Even a mild indication by the people with the most power that a certain individual or group are 'uncool' is life-changing.

Being at the bottom of the social strata is not much fun. I know because I've been there myself. A dynamic is created whereby even those who would not harbour any ill will towards someone like Anthony feel unable to interact with him for fear of 'contamination', jeopardizing their own fragile grip on the squash ladder of life.

Anthony's reaction to this state of affairs was not what you might expect. There was a reason that he was called 'the gentle giant'. He decided to use his Achilles heel to protect others in similar situations. He didn't fall into the usual survival cycle where the bullied eventually becomes the bully in an attempt to right the wrongs perpetrated on them. He used what he had learnt to look after the people whom he knew were even more vulnerable than he was. So he could regularly be seen helping really small kids and he proudly told people that he would one day like to work helping elderly people with their day-to-day lives. This beautiful giving nature had been developing in him at the same time that he was developing a connection with a local church youth group. He and his mother had chanced upon an open-air event on their village green and started to get involved.

During the days that led up to the concert, he knew that something was stirring in him. The band had caused quite a buzz in the area, so playground conversations contained the unusual collision of pop and God. Were these guys just using their 'message' to get into schools and sell CDs to impressionable kids? Were they really that good anyway? Did they have a record deal? How soon would they be on *CD:UK*? Do you really think they believe all that God stuff, or has someone put them up to it? Do you think the lead singer could really be a Christian, 'cos she's actually pretty fit? Anthony had listened in on many such conversations, but to no one's surprise, had not contributed to the discussion. The difference was that, for once, he trusted that his internal dialogue was probably more meaningful than what he'd been hearing in the playground. Would they really come to Hornchurch if they were trying to make it big? Could they really have made up all those stories about how God had changed their lives? If they weren't serious, would they really get up at 6.30 a.m. to put that PA up without getting paid for doing it? But there's only so much I can tell you about what was going on inside Anthony's head. More than anything else, he was entranced that these people seemed to be connecting with someone or something whose presence was reliable, and who accepted everyone as they were. 'Accepted' was not a word that Anthony had understood for a long time.

Friday night arrived. The lights glared and the music played. Anthony would later say that it was the most important night of his life, but if you'd been watching him during the concert you wouldn't have necessarily jumped to that conclusion. As the frenzied crowd bounced as one to the sound of hi-energy rock, he was hovering nervously off to the side with a couple of other conscientious objectors.

Ironically, it's often the folks standing at the sides of a venue whose faces you can actually see during a concert. When looking straight ahead your eyes are blinded by the spotlights and simply peer into the darkness. But stray window and emergency-exit light tends to fall on the faces of those on the perimeter of a gathering. I could definitely see the listening eyes of Anthony Brown. He would later talk about pennies dropping and jigsaw pieces falling into place, but to be honest, you wouldn't have known that from his demeanour. Again, I should stress that there's only so much I can really tell you about that.

That year much of our communication was based around telling the story of the Prodigal Son. It took various forms. Sometimes it would be a Jerry Springer show where young people could fire questions or comments at the different characters from the story. 'How could you just let him just breeze back in like that?' Sometimes it took the form of modern versions of the parable where a teenager nips off to London with his dad's credit card, which his dad keeps paying off, as it's his only way of following where his son has gone. The power of the story takes over. Unconditional love is so alien to so many young people today that they can actually fear it as something freakish. They only experience 'I'll love you for as long as I find you attractive', 'I'll love you for as long as you behave', 'I'll love you for as long as you make me laugh' and 'I'll love you for as long as you get good grades'. So when someone comes along saying, 'I love you. Full stop.' – it takes more than a little bit of processing.

That night, towards the end of the concert, I could sense the tangled stories of the young people in that room beginning to straighten out as they connected with this story of God. But bearing in mind how far beyond their radar these concepts are, there is a massive difference between hearing about it, and actually experiencing it. What I have had the privilege of seeing is so many young people stepping right into this story and meeting the perfect Father. Only when they step into this story can they get away from the baggage of their own life situations, where unconditional love has been pretty thin on the ground, and where 'father' has often been just a concept, not a reality.

At the end of my talk I invited people to stretch out their arms if they wanted to turn around, come home and receive the embrace of an all-loving, all-giving Father. Many of them did, and I could see that one of them was Anthony.

After the concert he came straight across to Darren (the youth worker who had organized our week) and myself and asked us to pray with him. He explained everything that had been running through his head all week, and how desperate he was to connect with God. Both our hearts were breaking as he shared about his struggles around other young people, both inside and outside school. But our hearts were leaping as he then spoke to God with a confidence and a passion that would have convinced you that he had been doing it for years. I think in his own way, he had. We felt we had shared something special in praying with and for this beautiful man-in-waiting. He went home very happy.

Four months later, I randomly bumped into Darren at a festival. He came bounding over to me, and after a customary embrace, fixed me in the eyes. You got the sense that this wasn't going to be your bog-standard reminiscing conversation.

'How is everyone getting on?' I asked.

'Well, there's some good news and some bad news,' Darren said. He went on to explain how Anthony had thrown himself into worship, Bible study and relationships on a level that he hadn't experienced before. He was telling people that he had never been happier than at this point of his life. The knowledge of being loved for who he was was freeing him to be himself with the people around him. The experience of being loved was changing the way he looked at himself in the mirror in the morning. Those who knew him reported that he had a new sense of purpose about his life, and a desire to share what had happened to him. He had even led a section of a youth group meeting just three weeks after the gig. He didn't, however, become any cooler.

'So not much bad news then?' I joked happily.

Darren stopped me in my tracks. 'Anthony died four weeks after the gig, Andy.'

Silence. More silence.

'You're joking, Darren,' I whispered.

He really wasn't. It seemed as if every emotion possible swept through my tired body. *What?!* That just doesn't happen, does it? He had been rushed into hospital with the sudden onset of a headache and uncontrollable vomiting. These were symptoms caused by a brain tumour that must have been working its way through his grey matter for some time. It had gone undetected, then suddenly burst an artery, causing massive brain damage. His vicar was called to the hospital at 1 a.m. to be with Anthony and his family. They then had to make the painful decision to turn off the life-support machine that was keeping Anthony alive. Grasping his hand, his vicar had the privilege of speaking the last words that Anthony would hear in this world. 'The next time you wake up, we'll all be with you again in a better place.'

What do you say at a moment like that? I was simultaneously praising and screaming at God. 'Why did you let that happen?... But thank you that he met you just in time... Thank you, thank you, thank you...' As the words bounced around my head, some perspective began to descend. I began to realize the awesome privilege of what Darren and I had been allowed to share in, and the crucial importance of it. Four weeks, Lord – that's cutting it fine. Our stories had for a short time run parallel with someone else's short story. However, that by itself wouldn't have been enough to change a life for the better and to change someone's eternal destiny. That simply happened because his story had connected with God's story.

You see, that's why there's only so much I could tell you about Anthony's story. I never had the opportunity to find out any more from the horse's mouth. But there is one important thing that I really can tell you. I know where he will be spending forever and, more importantly, who he'll be spending it with.

I'm pretty sure he'd want me to ask you, 'Will you be joining him?'

Youth For Christ (YFC) is a nationwide movement that was founded by Billy Graham in 1946. He dreamed of mobilising young Christians to reach their peers with the good news about Jesus Christ. Sixty years on, we remain committed to this vision, pursuing the most innovative means of communicating the gospel. YFC are hard at work in school classrooms, on football pitches, in skate parks and town centres, and even behind the walls of young offender prisons – working with unchurched teenagers.

We go further and we go first – using music, theatre, film, sports and new-media technology to reach 71,000 young people every week. From the Shetland Islands, right down to the Isle of Wight, YFC reach youth from every background. We are able to go to where young people are, communicating the good news relevantly to teenagers with no connection to the church – including young offenders and more challenging young people. This is so vital, at a time when 85% of people find faith before their 19th Birthday, and youth issues often dominate the news headlines. As well as introducing teenagers to the Christian faith, Youth For Christ's youth workers and church resources give young people a sense of self-worth and lifelong purpose. We invest in young people and see their behaviour transformed as a result. YFC are seeing young lives changed, nurturing tomorrow's leaders, and equipping young people with a heart for mission. We would greatly value your partnership at this key time.

To find out more please visit *www.yfc.co.uk*